FLOWER
PHILOSOPHY

FLOWER
PHILOSOPHY

*Seasonal projects
to inspire & restore*

Anna
Potter

*of Swallows
& Damsons*

WHITE LION
PUBLISHING

AUTUMN
98

WINTER
138

INTRODUCTION

Live in each season as it passes;
breathe the air, drink the drink,
taste the fruit, and resign yourself
to the influence of the Earth.

Henry David Thoreau

The sheer joy on my son's face when he reached into his jumper pocket and clutched in his grubby hand a solitary open flower. Soft and clumsy with tenderness and curiosity.

'IT BLOOMED IN MY POCKET!'

And surely that is all there is. As adults we encounter struggles, hurdles and barriers that, one by one, we must identify, challenge and overcome so that, as we watch them melt away, we can return to what lies within each one of us: all-encompassing joy, wonder and freedom. This is what nature so obviously and obnoxiously calls on us to do – to pay attention, to let go and to listen to the deep longing we have to connect with the wild.

Flower Philosophy comes as a follow-on from my first book, *The Flower Fix*, in which I focused on the aesthetics of floral design and the choices made to suit an environment. With this book I have chosen to head in a new direction, to reveal my inner thoughts in relation to the projects I create. My wish is to focus on a return to the untamed and to show how working with flowers can also serve as meditation, ritual and art.

In writing this book, I have explored industrial city, suburban maze, country village and the wild moor. By briar, bramble, robin and heron, I have observed how nature thrives and entwines and connects. I have watched busy humans interact, speed up, slow down. And I have listened to people talk of their days without taking a breath. What I have learned is that many of us seem endlessly to strive for perfection, which we all know deep down is unachievable. Through my watching and listening, I have gained new insights into the world around me simply through observing. But really observing. Not just looking and seeing, but seeking out the magic in small things. Not shying away from the unknown, from the shadows. I have discovered a powerful place in which we are all one, and this has been my inspiration for writing this book.

I should point out that my books are not strictly instructional 'how to' guides. You should feel free to use the ingredients lists and methods of arranging loosely. Following Constance Spry's model, the instructions simply make a good starting point from which you can develop your own creations, add your own stamp, create freely.

Journey Back to Nature

The freedom to create without unhelpful comparison is a hard turn to navigate right now. We are bound by the stories we are peddling, the things we pay attention to, the media, culture, our expectations, our perception of success, the pressures we lay on ourselves to post picture-perfect experiences on social media without ever actually having fully experienced it. We live as robots, plugged in, surrendering our inner spaciousness by running from one deadline, goal or crisis to the next. We latch on to things that fill up a schedule in order to tick our productivity quota. We are holding on so tightly to the transient and becoming ever more separate from the natural world and from one another. The mountains, woodlands, oceans and overgrown roadsides are calling us home. I see it in my dreams; I am being held by a giant mossy hand, or suspended in thick inky black water. Our tired, restless bodies are telling us that wildness is a necessity.

I write not as an expert, not to provide answers, but as a student, ever learning and documenting my findings in the hope that you, too, might find an opening or hear a calling that inspires you to ask your own questions. Journey back to nature, sit for a while, and soon she will dwell within you. Let her rot your name, decompose your history and make light of your daily chores. Let her put dirt under your nails, brambles in your hair and muddy your knees. Awaken your wild self, your innate poetry.

Seasonal Offerings

The arrangements in this book are arranged by season. An unavoidable cliché, perhaps, but I do not think so. During the lockdown months of previous years, I found myself surrendering to the rhythms of the natural world, from which we are not separate but very much a part of. I began writing in a frosty January garden, three blankets, two jumpers and one hot-water bottle thick, with a fire and a chai close by. Being dripped on as the flames beside me thawed the ice overhead, it felt necessary to be right there in that moment, listening.

As we learn to better understand what each part of the year has to show us and practise living within her cycles, it becomes easier to recognize moments of transition within ourselves. We may be experiencing summer physically, but deep inside, perhaps there is a need to winter. Life through the pandemic made me observe the time passing more closely, acutely aware of the changes in the season, and in myself. But it also led me to become intrinsically familiar with the flow of each season, to pay more attention to what was growing at any one time. It made me more curious, invited me to explore and experiment and encouraged me to practise gratitude and reciprocity.

Sustainability

I should like to add a note about sustainable practice, and how important it is as an industry – even as an individual who is simply experimenting with flowers – to take small steps to minimize a harmful impact on the planet. Seasonal, locally grown flowers are always the best option. Research your sources and find out how your flowers are grown and harvested. If buying locally grown is not an option – say, for seasonal reasons – find out where your flowers are imported from. Are they dyed? What are the conditions like on the farm

they have come from? Actively seeking this kind of information enables you to make a conscious decision on whether or not to buy flowers. Of course there are always dried flowers too, which have the added beauty of being reusable. Dry your own or buy dried from a supplier.

Another practice that is overlooked when considering sustainability is foraging. However, cutting even small amounts of vegetation from overgrown pathways or abandoned car parks could have a negative impact on the planet, so when it comes to taking from nature, always ask questions and be responsible with what you are taking, and how. Where is the best place to cut the stem? Is it better to remove from the root? Does a chosen plant have seedheads that you are spreading in a damaging way? How can you give back? The American Professor of Environmental and Forest Biology, Robin Wall Kimmerer, shared her perspective on restoration and reciprocity in *Braiding Sweetgrass*. She explores our relationship to the land, which is so often

one of taking, and encourages us all to consider how we might reciprocate the gifts given by Mother Nature. If you are unsure what a plant is, how it grows, its relationship to those around it and whether it is considered to be an invasive species, it may be better to leave it alone.

I hope that the exercises in this book can be used to cultivate gratitude, to accept and sit with the beautiful dualities of life and death, light and shadow. I want you to feel more than a deep connection to the wild; I want you to know it as one. Wherever you are, however rich, poor, lonely or satisfied, in city or in meadow, full of spring hope or deep winter longing, may the soft pink sunrise melt your hard corners and the robin soothe their sharp edges with her song. Let the dandelion nourish and the fermenting compost renew. May the silence of the heron quiet your breath and may you remember just how much you belong.

SPRING

This morning, before dawn, twilight in sight.
Stirring, I heard. Spring calling at the first mention of light,

Telling tales of dark stumble in hollow, crag and snow,
The journey of friends, mycelium, root, rot and marrow.

As they travelled the harshest known dirt underlands,
Their bond nourished the ground that we now hold in our hands.

Together their song was sung, through feather, fur and fern,
Heard on the wild north wind that nurtures and carries the tern.

So I nestled into blossom arms to drink in her news,
The next chapter, shedding coats, soft yellow hues.

Saluting the dirt where new shoots grow,
Weaving green hope that soon become meadow.

She sang 'Come tend, listen, to the murmuring ground',
From scented narcissi to the tubers that drowned.

In garden, moor, forest and city,
The song on the breeze, is spring's simple ditty.

Spring is a season of celebration, a time to welcome new life and growth and to give thanks for all that nature has to offer.

SPRING MUSINGS

It was wild intuition that made me look up when I did. It was a freezing cold March day – the kind on which you are definitely not wearing enough layers for hope of spring. Yet, as sure as the darkest hour comes just before dawn, the coldest hour, on this occasion, was just before spring. Soaring high above me were two herons. Elegant and purposeful. I had nowhere I needed to be other than wherever they were headed.

A few minutes from my house lies a pond secluded by big old trees, not known to many. I, like the herons, fell for it during the lockdown weeks of the Covid pandemic. With ever more people gathering in parks, for those shy creatures who feel a little raw, who prefer quiet solitude to nattering in groups, the pond is a small slice of still.

There is a tiny hut on this quiet pond with its heron and mallard and coot. A hut that has heard the grumbles of surprised fishermen, that is cosy with hot-water-bottle heat, flasks of tea and a pile of blankets. It is in this place that I come to write, about listening and following nature, returning to wild intuition that has been buried for fear of what might be unleashed. I find spring is a time where I start to feel a calling, a certain unease in the pit of my stomach that wants to break through and grow. I feel the urge to start something new and spend as much time as possible outside. To take risks – there is always a risk when something emerges from underground into the light.

Rituals

Bringing nature into the home at this time can be a source of real comfort and inspiration. Combining blossoming branches and bulb flowers with the past season's dried twigs, seedheads and moss lends a harmonious balance between the old and the new. Each is imbued with added beauty and meaning.

Every year I look forward to revisiting rituals that I have adopted over time. I make a spring wreath, either from scratch or by rejuvenating my dried Christmas wreath. There is poetry in combining the fresh, sometimes fleeting, spring blooms with scrappy and withered foliage and flowers that have dried out from seasons past. There's something very *wabi sabi* about it – the Japanese ethos that teaches us nothing lasts forever, nothing's perfect and nothing is ever finished.

I collect sprigs of foliage, blossom and twigs from my garden or I forage them while out on a walk, gathering these new ingredients together. Sparingly, I snip blossoming lengths of blackthorn, forsythia and spirea, and amelanchier, with its gnarly black stems. I fill old dishes with blossom and miniature daffodils or grape hyacinths, all scented and fleeting. I craft arrangements of tulips, learning to work with their bent and shapely forms.

Seasonal Transitions

More than any other season, spring is characterized by contrast. Early on, all is stark as new shoots take their time to grow. It is a time marked by newness, shoots, blossom and firsts. Snowdrops, daffodils, bluebells and forget-me-nots. These are the flowers of my childhood, laced through knee-deep ivy in the woods at the back of my house; a full immersion in faeriedom. I can still recall walking barefoot through the garden in spring, the cold dew feeling at once uncomfortable and familiar, strangely comforting.

Mid-spring, unassuming streets at any other time of the year, with their rows of terraced houses, become alive with the most magnificent cherry blossom. They mark where we are in the year with their blooms, and the progression of spring in mere weeks with their debris. And then, before you know it, it's full-on verdant intoxication. By late spring we are immersed in lush, wet, green foliage – peonies, irises, bats and swallows.

The subtlest of shifts, the simplest of occurrences, can be reminders of nature's ever-changing landscape. For me, late spring is often realized when the bats are back. Tiny, mysterious and erratic, they fill me with childlike curiosity. Somewhere between a large moth and a bird, the bat dives in circles that look totally nonsensical, and I cannot help but wonder if it has a precise pattern as to its path. When I was a child I would wait until sunset in spring and summer and race up to my parents' bedroom at the front of the house, its windows wide enough that at least four of us could stand and watch. Just as the sky turned from a vivid daytime blue to nighttime blue and trees are no longer green, but shadows – that is the bat hour.

Out they would emerge from the monkey puzzle tree in our garden, and perform their routine. Up, down, loop the loop, swoop in a circle and repeat. Occasionally one would misjudge or go rogue and fly straight into my parents' window. The drama and excitement, the evenings getting longer, more time for playing outside.

My Inner Gardener

As I sow seeds in preparation for the summer circus of blooms, I can feel the seeds within myself stirring, like a midwife of the soul waiting to create and birth something new. Working with my hands in the bare soil, I'm so deeply attentive to where space has been cleared over winter, ready for areas of growth. As the brave buds swell and risk baring all in complete vulnerability, I, too – an ever-enthusiastic student of life – realize that perhaps I am here to blossom, that the courage it takes to step into fullness is part of the season's rhythm.

As sowing the seeds requires preparation, it dawns on me that this is what winters are for: clearing the old and feeding the dirt. And then there is the activity itself, the physical act of planting. As someone who struggles to see projects through to completion, or even simply to pick one viable option from the overwhelming number of ideas I have every day, I apply this method of planting seeds to my daily life. What am I hoping to grow? How long will it take? What conditions will it need? When is the best time to start? How does it fit with everything else? And where best will it be seen and appreciated? It provides this unruly wildling with a framework within which to act and thrive.

Many gardeners keep meticulous charts of things they grow, keeping notes to record what has worked well and what has not. Would it be too much, do you think, to keep some kind of record like this for myself? A chart of ventures tried, relationships had, emotions expressed. An inner gardener of mind, body and spirit, starting with the simple act of planting a seed.

SPRING

COLLECTION

SEASONAL WREATH

Harvested out in the wild, the ingredients for this arrangement become a fusion of darkness and light, of life and death. By letting go of the old ways we can truly, creatively, make way for something new.

During the Covid-19 pandemic I felt frustrated by its limitations. How could I create now that I was no longer able to select flowers from a fully stocked market? And yet, looking around me, I saw so very much beauty, such wealth that, before now, I had simply overlooked. So, I began to tread the path unknown, finding novel materials to work with on quiet spring walks, and this has since become a ritual for me. I seek out new materials purely for colour, texture and movement, and not because I've seen them somewhere on Instagram or because they are the latest fashionable bloom.

And, so, to the stems for my wreath. Cherry, or Portuguese, laurel is often relegated to car parks and neglected areas of our gardens. Left without vigorous pruning, it produces the sweetest-smelling cascading blossoms. The leaves have the most deliciously inviting almond fragrance, yet they contain poisonous hydrogen cyanide. Having cut and used the blossoms unwittingly, I'm now drawn to this darker side that gives the plant a sinister beauty. Similarly, the blackthorn blossom – possibly my favourite of all the spring-flowering branches – has its own library of dark tales and folklore, of witchcraft and sorcery. In some traditions, a long, hard winter is referred to as a 'blackthorn winter'. A common theme that runs through the old stories is that blackthorn helps us to face the inevitability of our own death.

Straight, sturdy stems of pussy willow are no strangers to a seasoned florist, who might use them in hotel displays or winter bouquets. I've never been interested in these rigid, pristine fluff-ball sticks, but what I find in nature challenges my prejudice, for here are beautiful, light, wispy branches of catkins dusted with messy pollen, translucent and ethereal, chartreuse in tone. Traditionally the first branch to be brought into the home in springtime or used in place of palms at Easter services, pussy willow is a symbol of new life and hope. Easter and the spring equinox both celebrate newness and life. The Earth returns to a place of perfect balance. Day and night are equal, the light and the dark bringing the return of some much-needed balance into our own lives.

Ingredients

Wire wreath frame measuring
*   30 cm (12 in) in diameter*
Roll of wreath wire
Strong scissors or secateurs
Moss
Laurel x 15 stems
Pussy willow x 12 stems
Ornamental pear x 10 stems
Hellebore x 10 stems
Blackthorn x 6 stems
Berberis x 6 stems
Forsythia x 3 large stems

Method

1. Attach the reel wire to the wreath frame by wrapping it around once or twice and tying a knot. Keep this fixed to the wreath for the entirety of the making – you will continue to wrap the wire around the frame as you add your stems (see page 190).

2. Add small clumps of moss to the base, securing each by wrapping with wire. Completely cover one side of the wreath with moss.

3. Work your way around the wreath base again, this time adding the foliage and sprigs of blossom. Make small, hand-sized bunches of your ingredients, lay them flat on the wreath and wrap just the bottom 2 cm (1 in) of stem tightly to the base.

4. In each bunch, try to have one longer stem of pussy willow or sprig of blossom to help create movement in the design. As you add more foliage, use each new bunch to cover the stems of the last.

5. As you work your way around the wreath, alternate the bunches so that one is positioned slightly towards the inner edge of the wreath, and the next slightly towards the outer edge. It is good to use the fuller, fluffier ingredients such as the berberis on the inner bunches. They will fill the space without encroaching into the centre circle too much and you'll be able to keep a simple round shape in the middle.

6. Once you have added your last bunch of ingredients, tie the wire off and cut the connection. Finish your wreath with a ribbon, a favourite piece of fabric or nothing at all.

A DAFFODIL REVIVAL

Spring's earliest blooms, time-honoured and graceful, rise up out of a neoclassical mantel vase. This impactful asymmetrical arrangement resists the urge to follow the lines of the vase's curvaceous form and is altogether more wild and free.

'Daffodowndilly
She wore her yellow
   sun-bonnet,
She wore her
   greenest gown;
She turned to the
   south wind
And curtsied up and down.
She turned to the sunlight
And shook her yellow head,
And whispered to
   her neighbour:
"Winter is dead".'

A.A. MILNE

Is there a more nostalgic flower than the daffodil? For me, daffodils conjure notions of floral church displays and roadsides in spring, vintage postcards and Cicely Mary Barker fairies. A childlike bloom, common and simple in structure, it is often overlooked as a contender for formal flower arranging.

So many poets and writers have described the beautiful simplicity of the daffodil. Shakespeare celebrates the 'flower that comes before the swallow dares', Wordsworth catches them dancing in the breeze and Housman laments their demise come Easter. Traditionally daffodils symbolize new beginnings, fertility, good luck and strength, their large glowing blooms radiating in huge groups, reflecting the sun's warmth and their own resilience in being among the first to emerge from the cold dark winter. The first sight of daffodils has long been thought to bring the viewer luck, and taking care not to trample them is said to bring abundance.

Despite this flower's unfailing annual appearance, I tend to hold swathes of daffodils in parks as a sacred sight; they are not to be picked! Every year, I grow half a dozen or so varieties for cutting and I find it difficult to extract them from the garden. There has been a narcissus revival in recent years. Where once they may have been considered just a cartoon-like flower, we now see many unusual varieties: salmon, pink, coral, peach, crisp white and, of course, yellow. Besides the classic trumpet shape are exquisite, rare, tropical-looking flowers with huge, incredible ruffles or double petals.

For this arrangement I chose a 1950s ceramic mantle vase that I've always been drawn to because of its unusual dimensions. It lends itself perfectly to my design. Proportions are key here. It is all too easy to make the mistake of keeping the size of the arrangement close to that of the vase, and to follow its shapely curves. However, over the many years I have experimented and battled with these vases, failing and trying again, I have come to realize that to go big and break the lines of its form leads to an overall more impactful arrangement.

Ingredients

Wide, shallow vase measuring
  35 x 15 cm (14 x 6 in)
Chicken wire measuring
  50 x 50 cm (20 x 20 in)
Wire cutters
Gardening gloves
Florist's pot tape
Strong scissors or secateurs
Forsythia x 10 stems
Prunus blossom x 10 stems
Hellebore x 10 stems
Daffodil x 25 stems, different varieties

Method

1. Cut a large enough piece of chicken wire to fill your vase, loosely scrunching it into place. Secure across the top with a few strips of florist's pot tape (see page 183). Fill the vase with water.
2. Next, create the outline for the arrangement using your tallest pieces of blossom first – in my case, forsythia and prunus. Establish the highest and the widest points in order to achieve the overall size and proportion of the arrangement in relation to the vase. I chose to create an asymmetrical design.
3. Once the proportions are set, you can fill in more of the middle space using multiple stems of blossom, including the hellebores and daffodils. Remember to keep the overall shape of your arrangement intact.
4. Staying within the perimeter guide that you have set with the blossom branches, take care to use blooms with height higher up in the design and any shorter stems tucked in closely to the vase near the centre. Allow some of the longer stems to jut out at the sides.
5. Create varying depths with the blooms by having some tucked in and others protruding out in front of them, even if it feels as if they are obscuring the shorter blooms.
6. Weave any remaining smaller flowers, such as hellebores, in between the daffodils or wherever there may be a noticeable gap. Stand back from your arrangement to see if there are any lines you wish to break by having a flower interrupt them.

FLOWER PHILOSOPHY / Spring

The ancient Greek myth about Narcissus, a handsome youth who was granted his good looks by the gods, is a well-known tale. Being immortal, his beauty was permanent, but only on the condition that he never tried to view his own reflection. Once, while Narcissus was hunting in the woods, a beauteous wood nymph named Echo fell desperately in love with him, but Narcissus cruelly rejected her. So consumed was she with sadness, that the gods were not pleased. The goddess Nemesis lured Narcissus to a shimmering lake. There, in his vain state, he was unable to resist gazing at his own reflection, and fell in love with himself. As he gazed, the divine penalty took effect, and he simply faded away. In his place sprang up the golden flower that bears his name today. Once again, mythology provides a darker side to what often appears to be nothing but sunshine.

SPRING WARDROBE

Here is a design in which organized chaos rules, with the haphazard placement of different kinds of blossom. Main flowers are kept to a minimum so as not to anchor the arrangement or force it into a certain structure. The focus here is on the practice of freely creating without the need to be precious. It is as much about the process as it is the end product.

Ever since I began my floral journey, setting myself challenges or out-of-the-box projects has been a constant practice in loosening up my tense and achy floral muscles. Occasionally, to turn up somewhere with no plan, no preconceptions, or even any real idea of what a space will be like can be a freeing exercise – simply arrive armed with buckets of blossom and some seasonal ingredients and see what happens.

On this occasion, my design made great use of the amelanchier in the garden that was close to shedding its flowers. Otherwise known as shadbush or juneberry, amelanchier has many more wholesome properties than just the glorious blossom on gnarly black stems against the backdrop of new rust-brown leaves. After the flowers come tasty, dark purple berries (juneberries) that look much like blackcurrants. Their flavour is similar to that of a blueberry or blackberry, only much sweeter with a crisp texture reminiscent of their relatives, apples and pears. In autumn the leaves transform into the most glorious shades of orangey reds and salmon pinks. There is so much variation and drama in a tree small enough for even the tiniest urban garden. Used in this installation, there is great movement in the way that each stem interacts with the next, and an explosion of scent – a sweet, honey-like fragrance that exudes new spring growth.

On a practical note, I am not suggesting that you fill your wardrobe with flowers for one highly impractical and lavish moment of creativity! This project simply serves as an insight into what can be achieved and imagined when allowing yourself the space and time to play for no reason other than feeding an inner vitality. However, this style of arrangement could be used to line an aisle at a wedding or on stairs in a home for an impactful and ethereal effect.

If your arrangements are going to be placed somewhere they are likely to get knocked and you want to avoid water spilling onto the floor, use wet moss inside the container in place of water.

Ingredients

Garden planters* measuring
    40 x 15 x 15 cm
    (16 x 6 x 6 in) x 6
Chicken wire measuring
    50 x 50 cm (20 x 20 in)
    x 6 pieces
Wire cutters
Gardening gloves
Florist's pot tape
Strong scissors or secateurs
Spirea x 30 branches
Amelanchier x 18 branches
Cotoneaster 'Peking' x 30 stems
Bog myrtle x 12 stems
Daffodils x 15 stems
Fritillaria persica 'Green
    Dreams' x 6 stems

* Plug any holes with a sealant or
waterproof lining

Method

1. Start by preparing your planters. Cut pieces of chicken wire slightly longer than each planter and scrunch it loosely inside the containers. Use florist's pot tape across the top of each planter, in two or three different places, to secure the chicken wire (see page 184). Fill each planter two-thirds full with water.

2. Divide your ingredients roughly between your planters and start by placing the tallest stems. Use the spirea branches to create light, wispy shapes and an overall wild effect in the design.

3. Rather more bushy, owing to their coppery leaves and clusters of blossom, use the amelanchier branches to bring more height and movement to the design, but also to fill out any gaps areas among the spirea stems.

4. Using the taller stems creates obvious holes lower down in the design, around the base of the container. The brownish-red cotoneaster 'Peking' is perfect for filling here, with its beautiful wiggly stems.

5. Combined with the cotoneaster, the bog myrtle brings a rusty tone into the design that blends in with the immediate surroundings and with the containers, tying them together in a harmonious flow.

6. Now add in the few flowers allocated for this arrangement. The daffodils lend a barely-there look to the design, with their translucent petals and soft, subtle, salmon centres.

7. Finish the design with *Fritillaria persica* 'Green Dreams', weaving its glorious bendy shapes in between the blossoms to bring a fresh, zingy green pop to the design.

TULIP MANIA

This arrangement is a fitting celebration of the tulip – heroine of the Dutch Golden Age – captured fleetingly in a portrait that is reminiscent of the Grand Masters.

'*A tulip doesn't strive to impress anyone. It doesn't struggle to be different than a rose. It doesn't have to. It is different . . . there's room in the garden for every flower.*'

MARIANNE WILLIAMSON

When the Netherlandish botanist Carolus Clusius planted his collection of tulip bulbs – a gift from the ambassador to Suleiman the Magnificent of Turkey – he found that the plants were able to tolerate the harsher climate and conditions of the Low Countries. The event is widely accepted as marking the beginning of the tulip's popularity in Europe, with the flower coming to symbolize the Dutch Golden Age. Tulips were unique from other flowers known to Europe at the time, because of their intense colour, intricate lines and exotic, flame-like streaks on the petals. The flower rapidly became a coveted luxury item, and a profusion of varieties followed.

Tulips are unique for their utter waywardness; these blooms just will not be manipulated. I have spent years trying to control them, taking advice from others and applying tricks found on the internet to stop them from growing in the vase and flopping over. I have pin-pricked their stems, added pennies to vases, wired them straight. I have turned them around in arrangements and have cut them down – 'this is how you look your best, tulip, now conform and everyone will like you' – all to no avail. Perfectly curated tulip arrangements have changed dramatically overnight, with stems crossing each other in a disorderly manner, some becoming too tall for the design and others – originally cascading perfectly over the side of the vase – now bending upwards, straining awkwardly towards who knows what. But this is what tulips do best, these wild-spirited dancers.

And so, to this arrangement. When I haphazardly planted tulip bulbs far too late in the season last November, I had no way of knowing just what a gift and soul balm these would turn out to be. I'll spend time carefully assessing the length of each stem, its curves, the shape of its bloom, I'll create a perfectly curated ballet with extensions, pirouettes and silhouettes. But I shall leave them some room to move and twist and turn. For these flowers didn't grow through winter and break through the ground to be restrained and moulded into something they are not. They are free and wild and know exactly what they want to do. It's changeable and unexpected and there's nothing you or I can do about it.

Ingredients

Large ceramic bowl measuring
 25 x 12 cm (10 x 5 in)
Chicken wire measuring
 30 x 30 cm (12 x 12 in)
Wire cutters
Gardening gloves
Florist's pot tape
Strong scissors or secateurs
Amelanchier x 3 branches
Spirea x 10 branches
Large tulip x 25 stems (I used 'La Belle
 Époque', 'Copper Image', 'Brownie',
 'Cairo', 'Brown Sugar' and 'Palmyra')
Garden rose x 2 stems
Ranunculus x 3 stems
Oxypetalum x 6 stems
Grape hyacinth x 5 stems
Fritillaria uva-vulpis x 6 stems

Method

1. Cut a piece of chicken wire that is larger than your vessel and scrunch it into a ball shape that fits snuggly inside. Use florist's pot tape to secure it (see page 184). Fill the vessel with water.
2. Starting with a few branches of blossom, spirea or amelanchier, create the broad outline of your arrangement, capturing the highest points and the widest points.
3. Choose the longest tulips and consider their bends, their shapes, the direction of their curves, and use these stems to accentuate the shape that has already been formed with the foliage branches. I take off the majority of the leaves in order to focus on the flowers and not busy up the arrangement with too much green.
4. Tuck the remaining large-headed flowers in between the shortest blooms and the tallest tulips. Place them at varying depths, to prevent the arrangement taking on a flat appearance. This will also allow the tulips to move, change shape and grow in the vase.
5. Any very short-stemmed rose or ranunculus blooms can be tucked in closer to the chicken wire around the centre and rim of the container.
6. Once all the main flowers are positioned, you can weave in the smaller sprigs – the oxypetalum, grape hyacinths and *Fritillaria* – to fill any gaps and bring colour to the darker areas. Allow some of the more delicate stems to drape down, cascading over the side of the vessel.

ANCIENT WISDOM

A rather battered urn makes the ideal pairing for gnarled and twisted magnolia stems. In this arrangement, the earthy tones of 'Brownie' and 'Cairo' tulips mix with the muted blush tones of 'La Belle Époque', while bog myrtle gently echoes the warm browns in the tulips.

'We should bow deeply before the orchid and the snail and join our palms reverently before the monarch butterfly and the magnolia tree. The feeling of respect for all species will help us recognize the noblest nature in ourselves.'

THICH NHAT HANH

Magnolia is a bloom that you just cannot buy from the market. They are available, of course, but they do not have the majesty of stems you see on living trees. These trees need time and space to mature, and that is not an equation that works for a successful flower-growing business, which is more about getting as many flowers as possible in a short space of time. I only tend to get hold of these golden ingredients by tentatively asking friends or staying alert to see if any local trees are being pruned.

Magnolias are thought to be one of Earth's first flowering plants. Fossil remains show that species have been around for at least 20 million years, all following the same blueprint. Evolving before there were bees, they relied on beetles to pollinate them. Because these beetles are interested only in pollen, the flowers mature to allow for cross-pollination. The male parts develop first and offer up their pollen, followed closely by the female parts. These produce no reward for the beetles but cleverly mimic the male parts, ensuring that the beetles are inquisitive in their exploration and pollinate the flowers in the process. Knowing that this has been going on for millennia – and long before humans inhabited Earth – is truly humbling.

Researching the meaning behind these flowers has led me to lots of different words about beauty and femininity and love. But there is also a thread that speaks of resilience, tenacity and strength. Given the species history, this seems wholly appropriate. Adaptation, questioning, wisdom, these words speak beyond glorious outer beauty to outlast a fleeting bloom.

This large urn is the perfect host for the magnolia branches I was so generously allowed to cut from a friend's tree. They were all wonky and of differing sizes – ideal for creating movement and overhanging shapes. To build an arrangement that was large enough, proportionally, to the old urn, I called on some tall stems of spirea blossom and amelanchier to accompany the magnolia. For a splash of colour, I used spring's first tulips from the garden, some reaching 1 m (3 ft) tall.

Ingredients

Large, rustic urn* measuring
    60 x 30 cm (24 x 12 in)
Chicken wire measuring
    75 x 50 cm (30 x 20 in)
Wire cutters
Gardening gloves
Florist's pot tape
Strong scissors or secateurs
Amelanchier x 10 branches
Spirea x 12 branches
Bog myrtle x 10 stems
Magnolia x 10 branches
Daffodil x 10 stems
Tulip x 15 stems (I used 'La Belle Époque',
    'Cairo' and 'Brownie')

* If your urn is very rustic, you may need
to find a second container that fits inside
it to ensure no water leaks out.

Method

1. Cut a length of chicken wire slightly larger than the urn and scrunch it loosely. Place the chicken wire inside the urn and secure with florist's pot tape (see page 184). Fill the urn with water.

2. Start to add the stems and blossoms that will create the height and width of your desired design. Use the tallest branches first, for height. I had a particularly majestic amelanchier branch, at least three times the height of my urn.

3. With the height established, fill out the width using the next tallest stems of amelanchier and spirea. It is important to create a set framework within which to build your design.

4. Should you have tall tulips with natural curves, add them in at this stage, and use shorter, curvy tulips around the bottom of the design, so that they hang over the side of the urn and give a beautiful asymmetrical and organic look. Place stems of coppery bog myrtle at the centre of the arrangement, and at the sides, to add texture and warmth to the overall design.

5. When it comes to adding the magnolia, do so in a way that will showcase the flowers while creating movement within the arrangement. Take care not to overcrowd any part of the arrangement with large blooms or dense areas of foliage.

6. Each stem is unique, and the gnarly branches may not go exactly where you intend them to. Simply work with these quirks and look at each stem individually to see where it adds most to the overall design. I find a lot of short magnolia stems, heavily weighted at one end with blooms, lend themselves perfectly to overhanging and cascading out of the arrangement.

7. I did not want to add too much in the way of flowers to my arrangement. I already had tulips in earthy shades to echo the coppery browns and rust in the bog myrtle. Adding in a few daffodils introduced a light movement to the overall design.

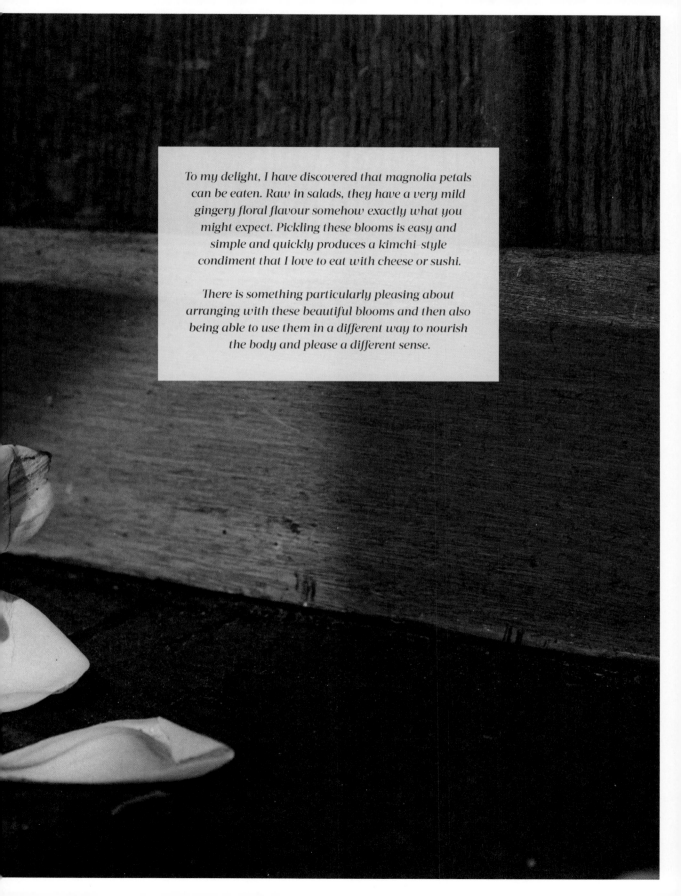

To my delight, I have discovered that magnolia petals can be eaten. Raw in salads, they have a very mild gingery floral flavour somehow exactly what you might expect. Pickling these blooms is easy and simple and quickly produces a kimchi-style condiment that I love to eat with cheese or sushi.

There is something particularly pleasing about arranging with these beautiful blooms and then also being able to use them in a different way to nourish the body and please a different sense.

BELTANE'S BLESSING

*Spring, Easter, Beltane – these are all
celebrations of life and growth and of marking a
change in season through ritual. Here, tulips,
peonies and ranunculus collide in a big blousy
petal party, peppered with lilac and violas, for a
seasonal tablescape and hand-tied bouquet.*

After years of creating detailed and flamboyant tablescapes for weddings
and events, paying attention to the finest details, the most subtle colour
combinations, and picking out elements in stationery with flowers or
matching a shade of candle to a variety of rose, it is fair to say I had become
weary when it came to setting a table for a gathering of my own. But with
the drought of events and gatherings over the past years I soon felt the desire
and longing to create again, to use seasonal ingredients in ways that reflected
the time of year, the collective feeling of togetherness, of celebrating life and
relationships. And what better time for this than in spring?

Blessed Beltane to you all!
Let's look to the blossoms and growth, rising with enhanced vigor.

When my oldest friend from across the ocean sent me this blessing,
I first thought it airy-fairy. But that word kept knocking on my door: Beltane.
Searching for its meaning, I discovered that, halfway between spring
equinox and summer solstice, this Gaelic festival celebrates the return of
fertility to the ground and the word itself, 'Beltane', loosely means 'bright
fire'. This transitioning time from spring to summer sees blossoms fleetingly
fall and new growth strengthen. Roots deepen and bulbs go back to the
earth to conserve their energy. This is the time to give thanks for all the
wealth that is to come.

In setting a table for a seasonal gathering, you can intensify your
intentions by weaving objects and other treasures into the scene. A colour
palette that evokes a certain energy or the scattering of seasonal fruits can
bring significant layers to the event. The meanings or herbal properties of
flowers are a good place to start. Peonies are abundance and richness, tulips,
deep love; lilacs are first love. Quail eggs, an ancient symbol of new life, have
long been associated with pagan festivals celebrating spring.

Ingredients

Shallow bowl measuring
* 18 x 10 cm (7 x 4 in)*
Chicken wire measuring
* 30 x 30 cm (12 x 12 in)*
Wire cutters
Gardening gloves
Florist's pot tape
Strong scissors or secateurs
Bud vases x 9
Quail egg or chocolate egg x 20
Candlestick and candle x 2–3
String
Ribbon
Sycamore x 8 small branches
Lilac x 7 stems
Tulip x 10 stems
Peony x 4 stems
Ranunculus x 16 stems
Geum x 6 stems
Viola 'Tiger Eye Red' x 10 stems
Golden smoke bush x 5 small branches
Spirea x 5 stems

Method: Tablescape

1. Prepare the centrepiece for your table. Cut a square of chicken wire that is about twice the size of your vessel. Scrunch the wire into a loose ball, place it in your vessel and secure over the top with a cross of florist's pot tape (see page 184). Fill the bowl with water.
2. Start with some sycamore foliage, to capture the overall shape of your design. I planned to have just one tall stem for the highest point of my table display. Have a few leaves cascading over the sides of the bowl, to give structure to the lower, draping part of the arrangement.
3. Follow the lines of your sycamore foliage to add some bushy stems of lilac around the base of the arrangement.
4. Choose and place your tallest stem – in my case, a tulip – and then place the largest blooms, the peonies, before the arrangement gets too crowded with other flowers. I placed one either side of my design, near the bottom and off-centre, to prevent them becoming too much of a spectacle. Placing them to the side and balanced out with other blooms helps create a more harmonious and natural feel to the arrangement.
5. Now add the other larger-headed flowers, including any remaining tulips and the ranunculas, at staggered heights that follow the shape already set by the foliage.
6. Finish the tablescape design with a few delicate geum stems, using them to fill any gaps in the arrangement.
7. Fill the bud vases with various heights of single stems – violas, tulips, peonies – and scatter eggs among the flowers along the table.
8. Add candles to your tablescape, to mirror the height of the tallest stems. Place the candles between the bud vases at either end of the table.

Method: Hand-tied Bouquet

1. For the hand-tied bouquet, start by creating an asymmetrical shape using sycamore, smoke bush and spirea. Five to six stems crisscrossed and held loosely will act as a frame for the whole bouquet.
2. Next add some lilac and your largest blooms. I try to keep a dip in the centre of the bouquet by tucking one flower a little further down than the others. Add some longer stems either side to elongate the shape.
3. At the front, keep the blooms fairly tucked in. Add the more delicate stems throughout the bouquet, with some of them protruding a little, to give movement and a more natural feel.
4. Tie the stems with string or twine, just above where you have been holding the bouquet. Wrap the twine around a few times, until you can ease the pressure of your grip, and tie into a knot.
5. Finish by wrapping a ribbon around the stems (over the string) and leaving the tails long to trail down.

BLOOM & FADE

This arrangement captures that sweet point towards the end of spring, where the last tulips are still in bloom and the garden is filled with the sweetness of lilac and viburnum blossom. It is neither one season nor another, it is May in all its glory; light and warm, inviting and transient.

The conversation started during photography – a simple question to India, my photographer, as to whether she considered peonies a spring or summer flower. You might think this an easy, breezy question but before I knew it, we had tumbled through deeper reflections on time and seasons, for flower philosophy is our strong point.

Tove Jansson talks about borders. Borders between seasons – spring/summer, autumn/winter. The lines between land and water, ground and sky. I've always felt drawn to these moments and spaces, the in-betweens. I have noticed within myself, when wild swimming, that the border between land and water acts as a door. The crossing from one to the other, the uncertainty. This newness momentarily shifts a small, limited perspective into something bigger; a gateway into now, the present moment. This applies to seasons, too. An unknown time between what is classed as one or the other is a border. For me, peonies have come to symbolize this quiet transformation. Peonies are a door. In the garden their buds slowly swell and voluptuously bloom and then are gone in an instant, leaving a big inky mess on the ground. Opening a door where once there was a wall.

Standing in this room with its faded, 1970s floral wallpaper as a backdrop to identical flowers that were blooming right then, in that very moment, brought new meaning to our discussion. Here were these flowers, replicating the patterns on the walls, with no knowledge of the season, or even the year. The conjuncture was almost too much to hold – the concept of a past that no longer exists, the passing of time that is like a millisecond in the whole existence of the universe. I could not help but feel a sense of our smallness and how short our time on Earth has been. So, now, instead of being quick to label what season I'm working in, which flowers belong where and why, I try to use this ambiguity as a way of embracing the unknown. Every time a new flower blooms all I really need to know is that it is happening right now.

'In this there is no measuring with time, a year doesn't matter, and ten years are nothing. Being an artist means: not numbering and counting, but ripening like a tree, which doesn't force its sap, and stands confidently in the storms of spring, not afraid that afterward summer may not come. It does come. But it comes only to those who are patient, who are there as if eternity lay before them, so unconcernedly silent and vast. I learn it every day of my life, learn it with pain I am grateful for: patience is everything.'

RAINER MARIA RILKE

Ingredients

*Shallow vase measuring
    15 x 15 cm (6 x 6 in)*
*Chicken wire measuring
    30 x 30 cm (12 x 12 in)*
Wire cutters
Gardening gloves
Florist's pot tape
Secateurs or strong scissors
Rose foliage x 2 stems
White lilac x 6 stems
Tree peony x 3 stems
Tulip x 12 stems (white and copper)
Viburnum blossom x 5 stems
Hellebore x 4 stems
Primula x 2 stems

Method

1. A project like this works best in a shallow container that is filled with chicken wire scrunched in a ball. Cut enough to ensure that the dome of wire is slightly higher than the rim of the vessel, to provide extra support for the tallest stems. Use florist's pot tape to secure the wire, creating a criss-cross of tape over the top (see page 184). Fill the vase with water.
2. The success of this arrangement relies on its shape within the wider environment. Take time to assess the space your flowers will occupy – how much space is there and what other vertical or horizontal lines do you need to consider? I opted for an asymmetrical design with the highest point – a rose stem – to one side.
3. After deciding on the highest point, give balance to your design by creating the lowest point on the opposite side. I tucked some lilac tightly into the vase, allowing a few stems to drape down over the side of the table.
4. Fill out the arrangement, working between the highest and lowest points to place the tallest blooms. I alternated between peonies and tulips here, tucking some in neatly, while allowing one or two to jut out of the design.
5. Around the lower section of the design, work to fill any gaps and create depth. I used more lilac to help me achieve this, as well as a few tulips and some viburnum.
6. Finish up by placing the more subtle flowers, the hellebores and primulas, among the lighter flowers, to add a little more depth and dimension, but without introducing anything that contrasts too heavily or conflicts with the wider environment – in this case, to blend naturally with the faded wallpaper.

SUMMER

I am not a poet
Nor do I know anything with the certainty of the changing seasons.

But I do feel. Deeply and lightly.
I am able, occasionally, to pull myself from the torrid business of doing
the dishes or to put down the heavy rucksack of roles that I
reluctantly carry around on my back.

It might be a child's playful smile or a quick game of peek-a-boo in the
bakery queue. Or the trees that stretch to greet each other from either
side of the road, plummeting us into darkness as we drive through a
dark green summer tunnel. It might be the scent of old roses, a door
into nowness.

I am sometimes able to tread lightly with these clumsy feet as I watch the
light disco-balling through the dressed-up trees, spotlighting
pavement dandelion clocks and other such thriving unworldly weeds.

I can also tend to the garden patiently, despite my hyperactivity, and make
cups of tea for the council of owl and fox and honeysuckle and let
them chatter together regardless of my habit of interrupting
conversations.

But still, I know very little. Perhaps that makes me more poet than not.

Summer is a season of rapid growth and abundance. This is the time to make hay while the sun shines, and to bathe in the warmth and light of longer days.

SUMMER MUSINGS

As the season approaches, I tell myself I am not so interested in summer all dressed up in its florals. Everybody's favourite time of year, it is always the obvious choice: plentiful, abundant, voluptuous. I wonder if the summer triggers some inner resentment I must hold. It's like the popular kid who always gets picked first for the team, the most talented and best looking. Surely the story of the underdog makes for the best movie? Everyone smiles when winter is made prom queen or gets the university scholarship, don't they?

Mixed Feelings

Certainly, the days are longer, but the time flies faster and the skies are louder. Jet planes and bees, birds and sirens. A climax of ripe nature and human frivolity. Summer evokes a longing that I, for some reason, have squashed and buried with my dahlia tubers. I yearn for the ease and simplicity of being outside from dawn until dusk, nights comfortable enough to really gaze at the moon. Summer legs, bruised and scraped; smooth feet, eroded by rock, gravel and sand. Long days laced with imagination and raspberries. The land mutters, 'Come take me, bathe and enjoy. Rest a while,' The flowers sing,

'Do not be afraid of your fullness; allow yourself to bloom and ripen.' Gradually, I succumb to the season's irresistible lure. There is a place in the long grass I find my summer home. A holiday house of broken golden light, dragonflies and dirt. The air dappled with otherworldly seed ghosts and flies. At last, I embrace the lightness. Eventually I take off my winter coat.

Any bitterness is soon sweetened by pollen, carried away in the sparrow's beak; softened by the heat like butter, held in the thick air. Reciprocate, reciprocate. A fruiting gift that is truly received nourishes our connection to Earth.

A Change of Pace

Within the blink of an eye, growth rates reach supersonic speeds in summer. The garden in its oh-so-pleasing, order suddenly becomes an overgrown, verdant jungle. Sprouting from every crevice, each tiny shoot holding the optimistic promise of being that bronze bupleurum that I sow every year and yet many a time another raspberry cane or dandelion appears.

The riverbank where I eat lunch has suddenly concealed all the tiny details I slowly ponder.

The robin, ducklings and mayflies all gone, a bright green blanket dotted with wasps in its wake. Grief for the small, quiet things felt, which is no less than a longing within me for slower and simpler days.

All those things packed into the 'holidays' – such a dangerous contradiction of terms. Work, no school, weddings, parties, clean, decorate, take that yearly break. Have fun, get things done, rest . . . I never quite know what to say at the school gates when asked seven times if I 'had a good summer'. Yes, no, sometimes. Perhaps it's just me that feels the strain of the warmer days, the pull to make hay while the sun shines and then collapse into a guilt-infused wallow of not stopping to appreciate it all. Why does no one ask, did you have a good autumn, spring or winter?

Soulful Surrender

Because the cycle of growth, bloom and death happens in such a short time in summer, I've found myself having to completely surrender to it or I so quickly feel like I'm trying to catch my tail and never quite reach the impossible.

Every year I find myself having to work at being OK with the overgrown mess, the imperfections, the weeds, the crispy brown bits, the long grass. More than feeling OK with these things, I want to express gratitude. Seeing the precious warm moments of stillness, the river water that stings a little less, the great heron keeping watch. The carefree dance of the swallows and ripe fruit. I want to embrace the abundance that desires us to look long and hard enough to see.

I accept what is. I feel the warmth, the lightness, the sun's energy and wild growth. This is a time for taking twilight strolls before bedtime, among the luminous night phlox and neon red hot pokers eerily highlighted in the pale blue light. It is a time for daytime journeys through moors transformed into a carpet of mauve that shifts the shape and form of the hills from cold, rugged and harsh into soft, inviting mounds. A place for

frolicking and play. What better for the soul than to languish in warmer waters that comfortably hold hot animal bodies, to take a night swim?

Here and Now

Summer has a way of really inspiring us to be present. Fleeting flowers in full bloom are just one hot day away from shedding their petals. Whether deadheading, watching the ground or staying on top of vigorous weeds, I am constantly aware that everything is happening right now. There's a tendency in other seasons to think ahead more . . . planting for summer in spring, and for spring in autumn. In winter? Dreaming of warmer days. But in summer, no. Make use of what you have while it lasts is the floral carpe diem for the season.

This is my favourite time of year for humble weeds and herbs: mugwort, dock, lemon balm and mint. As September approaches these plants bear stems and foliage that are firm enough to pick and last well in arrangements. This is the time to recreate wild meadows and country roadside landscapes. And while you are looking, use berries too! From young strawberries and raspberries early on in the season to the elderberries and blackberries at its close. Buttonholes with miniature strawberries for a summer wedding – one of the delicacies of the season. A quick snack après the 'I do's'!

And the best of the summer? After-dark hours outside are simply delicious. A fire and a blanket, a time for shy creatures and quiet humans. The rustle of fox and badger in the compost and the tawny owl in the nearby beech. My absolute favourite part of summer. Windows and heart open.

SUMMER

COLLECTION

SMOKE & GREY

'I thought the most
beautiful thing in the
world must be shadow.'

SYLVIA PLATH

*The sultry, shadowy mood of this arrangement
doesn't necessarily say 'summer', yet all of these
plants are in bloom at this time of year, creating
their own smoky haze on the longest of days.*

Sitting silently in my garden at the midnight hour, I hear the scuffles and
squeaks of nighttime animals. The soft glow of the fire lights a small circle in
front of me, the smoke shrouding the scene with a haze. Sometimes there is
such a keen sense of mystery that I want to bottle it so that I can pour it into
my art. It is made of colour and wonder and aliveness. Laced with a little fear
and solitude, it is rooted in darkness.

I sometimes struggle with light, bright, bold and breezy designs – not
only in flower-arranging, but in all disciplines. Contrary to Albert Camus'
popular 'invincible summer' quote, I find that in the depth of summer there
lies within me an invincible winter. Shadow work was a practice
popularized by psychologist Carl Jung, who used light and shadow to
explore the idea that all humans have a 'darker side'. I am all too aware that
humans have basic physiological needs that include feeling safe and secure,
and having a sense of belonging. They are inherent and instinctual.

As children, we have all bravely expressed certain parts of ourselves only
to find our behaviour deemed wrong, undesirable or shameful by others in
our environment. Maybe we got angry or acted spontaneously, boldly or
playfully at home or in the classroom and were punished or publicly scolded
for it. Such experiences threaten these basic needs.

I've found that self-expression, whether through painting, designing
with flowers or some other creative practice, often helps me connect and
channel these buried, shameful experiences. I find the act of transforming
such tucked-away feelings of being stigmatized into art is like taking baby
steps into acceptance and loving myself as a whole being. This plinth
arrangement was made as one of these expressions: to honour a darker side,
to live with the questions. To achieve the look I wanted, I teamed Amazing
Grey poppies with smoke bush and *Physocarpus opulifolius* 'Diabolo' in
full blossom. Punctuated with ammi and the few black and white 'Royal
Wedding' poppies that were open in my garden, the effect is to give a stormy
impression – soft, mystical and full of drama.

Ingredients

Heavy concrete pots measuring
18 x 16 cm (7 x 6¹/₄ in) x 2
Chicken wire measuring
30 x 30 cm (12 x 12 in) x 2
Wire cutters
Gardening gloves
Small bamboo canes, measuring
70 cm (28 in) each x 2
Florist's pot tape
Strong scissors or secateurs
Plinth
Smoke bush x 12 stems
Physocarpus opulifolius 'Diabolo'
x 10 stems
Poppy 'Amazing Grey' x 20 stems
Poppy 'Royal Wedding' x 5 stems
Ammi x 15 stems

Method

1. Prepare each container in the same way (see page 186): make a long tube of chicken wire, loosely scrunched, that fits snugly inside the neck of the pot. Slide a bamboo cane through the wire and into the pot to offer support. Secure the wire and the cane by fixing a couple strips of florist's pot tape across the opening of the pot.

2. Using a plinth allows you to create an arrangement with impressive height: place one pot on the plinth and the other on the floor in front of it. Tape the chicken wire of the lower pot to the plinth for extra stability. Fill each container with water.

3. Work with the tallest branches of smoke bush and *Physocarpus opulifolius* 'Diabolo' to gain the height you want in the arrangement. If the foliage you are using is of a variety that does not need to be in water, then you can use any length of stem for the highest parts. However, if it is a type of foliage that will benefit from being in water, the height of your arrangement will be determined by your longest stems.

4. With the height established, work down towards the neck of the pot to fill the chicken wire with more foliage.

5. At points along the way add the poppies in clusters, making sure their stems are in the water.

6. Use the blossoming ammi to create more width with its cloudlike bursts of white.

3

4

5

6

SUNBURST MANDALA

'I exist as I am, that is enough . . .'

WALT WHITMAN

Circles of summer arranged intuitively across the floor, this mandala-inspired design is led by the shapes and colours of the materials of its making.

I must have been making nature mandalas since I was about three years old, whether it be with shells, petals, freshly cut grass, feathers, conkers or bones. Creating shapes and patterns on the ground, cross-legged, knees bent, hunched over, rolling around – this is play at its simplest in a primal and childlike sense.

Every season has a different sweetshop of pick-and-mix ingredients. Winter has pinecones, branches, skeletal leaves. Spring holds new growth, tiny flowers from bulbs, blossoms. Autumn's cupboards are stocked with seedheads, crispy leaves, fruits. Summer is the most abundant, though, with its berries, leaves, blooms, weeds, young fruit on trees. For me, this time of year conjures memories of long, slow summer holidays in the garden, of annual childhood trips to north Wales and the North Yorkshire Moors, collecting, collecting, collecting. I would spill the contents of my pockets out onto the floor, arranging my precious jewels across the floorboards. Quartz, some crushed petals, an irregular pine cone, unripe blackberries, a sheep's femur bone and a nest of tangled wool caught on a hawthorn bush.

During rituals, a mandala can act as a spiritual guidance tool, employed to focus the participant's attention as a meditation practice. It is seen as a sacred symbol representing the essence of the universe. The name derives from two Sanskrit words, *manda* and *la*, which mean essence and container respectively and translate as 'circle'. In my arrangement, I've used the term quite literally and created circles inside of circles without too much mind thought or planning. Just as I did as a child, before I even knew anything of the sacred process of creating mandalas, I had a natural instinct to create in this way. You could say that I used my very essence to guide the design.

Ingredients

Floor space (preferably somewhere flat and not too windy)

Strong scissors or secateurs

Selection of flowers and foliage with contrasting shapes, sizes and tones; anything goes here, be guided by the season and the space in which you want to create

Method

1. Choose a flower or leaf for the very centre of your arrangement – something you might be particularly drawn to or that you have only one of. From this point, you'll be working outwards in circles, so make sure you have adequate floor space for your design.

2. Traditionally when mandalas are created a mantra is chanted, making it a beautiful tool for meditation practice. If the spirit takes you, say some soothing words as you build your circles.

3. Working your way outwards, place anchor points in the form of larger blooms, leaves or fruits, then use small-headed flowers to connect them together.

4. There really are no strict rules to creating a pattern in this way, as this is a mindful practice of pure self-expression.

5. Sweep the mandala away when you have finished, to signify impermanence, transience and life cycles.

SOLSTICE GATHERING

'The moon lives in the
lining of your skin.'

PABLO NERUDA

*Settling on the banks of a still lake, a group of
us gathered together one summer's afternoon.
To celebrate the summer solstice, and to
reinvigorate our connection with Earth, we each
made a crown from midsummer herbs before
gliding as one into the warm waters of the lake.*

For as long as I can remember, I have gravitated towards the longest and
shortest days. Markers in the year, in sunrises and sunsets, these days
reinforce the reliability of the seasons, steady and strong forces that contain
our complicated human dramas.

When I find myself with no diary space, every inch booked up and full
with this thing and the next, it makes me want to retreat and hide. With
nothing more to give, I become tired and unsociable.

When all feels too heavy and overwhelming, I set myself the task of
floating above this difficult, busy world and dancing to the rhythms of
nature. On this occasion, I found solace in a gathering of souls brought
together to create solstice crowns in nature, to make as the sun went
down on the longest day. For, in this moment, there were no pressures
of 'What do you do for a living?' or 'What special roles do you have?'

In the event, I notice the subtle and unspoken connection that forms
between people when they are together in nature, making, weaving,
observing, breathing in this shared experience. The energy is alive and
abundant, a space is created that is bigger than the physical environment
– some may even call it sacred. We weave and bind, laugh and pay attention.
The makings of a prayer. Each of us wears our crown like a uniform, a mark
of our belonging to the lake, the Earth and to one another. God, goddess,
there's no hierarchy here. As spiritual teacher Ram Dass would say, it's just
'souls, not roles'.

The summer solstice is a time for honouring our inner light. It is a time
to celebrate our connection to everything, to ignite and remember the fire
that keeps us alive; its abundance, its potential for growth. Named after Litha
– the goddess of fertility, power and order – we use symbolic midsummer
herbs to crown ourselves in nature (see page 79), to honour and connect to
the season and its warmth.

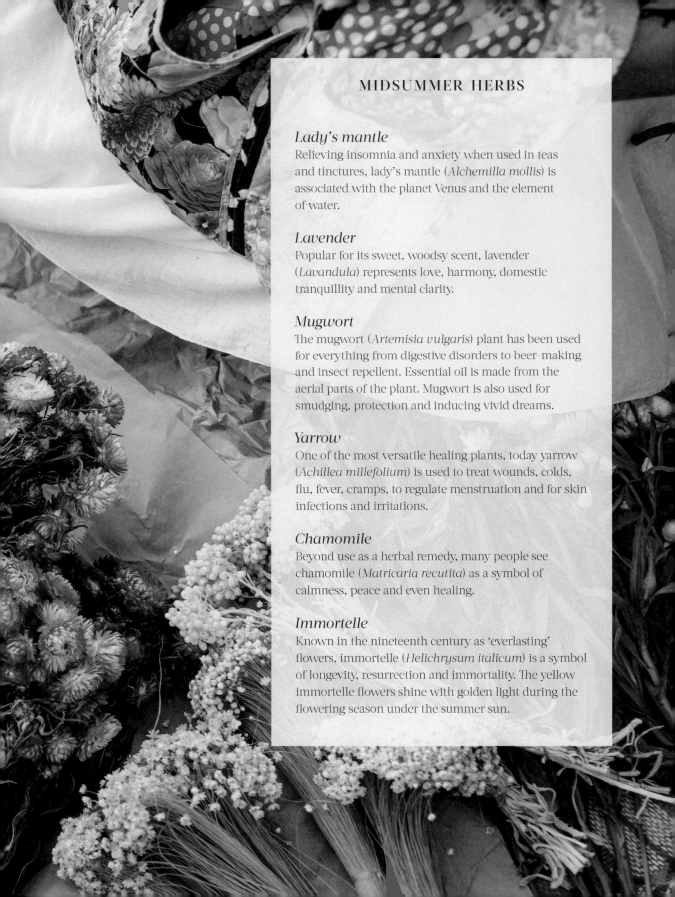

MIDSUMMER HERBS

Lady's mantle
Relieving insomnia and anxiety when used in teas and tinctures, lady's mantle (*Alchemilla mollis*) is associated with the planet Venus and the element of water.

Lavender
Popular for its sweet, woodsy scent, lavender (*Lavandula*) represents love, harmony, domestic tranquillity and mental clarity.

Mugwort
The mugwort (*Artemisia vulgaris*) plant has been used for everything from digestive disorders to beer-making and insect repellent. Essential oil is made from the aerial parts of the plant. Mugwort is also used for smudging, protection and inducing vivid dreams.

Yarrow
One of the most versatile healing plants, today yarrow (*Achillea millefolium*) is used to treat wounds, colds, flu, fever, cramps, to regulate menstruation and for skin infections and irritations.

Chamomile
Beyond use as a herbal remedy, many people see chamomile (*Matricaria recutita*) as a symbol of calmness, peace and even healing.

Immortelle
Known in the nineteenth century as 'everlasting' flowers, immortelle (*Helichrysum italicum*) is a symbol of longevity, resurrection and immortality. The yellow immortelle flowers shine with golden light during the flowering season under the summer sun.

Ingredients

*Flexible wire or vine as the base; it needs
to be slightly longer than the
circumference of your head*
Binding wire or twine
Strong scissors or secateurs
Lady's mantle x 5 stems
Lavender x 30 stems
Mugwort x 1 stem
Strawflower x 8 stems
Chamomile x 3 stems
Immortelle x 6 stems

Method

1. Starting at one end of your base wire, follow the steps for making a wreath (page 190) to attach small bunches of flowers. Use just three to five stems for each bunch.
2. Alternate the flowers from one bunch to the next, and lay each new bunch so that it covers the stems of the previous bunch. Secure just the stems to the base with the binding wire or twine.
3. Varying the lengths of the stems in each bunch will give your crown a more organic look, with some stems sticking out above the others.
4. At the very end, bring both ends together to form a circle. Secure, either by twisting the base wire or tying a knot.

PARKING LOT WEEDS

So often we pass by plants we consider weeds without seeing the beauty or value they so generously offer to us. A celebration of the overlooked and unwanted, this arrangement captures the spirit of plants we see huddled in the corners of parking lots, forcing their way out of the cracks in concrete pavements and thriving on roadside verges.

'Here we are
running with the weeds
colors exaggerated
pistils wild
embarrassing the calm
   family flowers
oh here we are
flourishing for the field
and the name of the place
is love.'

LUCILLE CLIFTON

Mugwort, dock, valerian, rosebay willow herb. Our bathroom cabinets and kitchen cupboards might be filled with pellets and nuggets and oils in bottles or teas derived from these healthful plants, yet we consider them a menace in the wild, intrusive and overgrown.

Over the centuries mugwort has been valued for its magical, mystical and spiritual uses, especially for inducing dreams and clairvoyance. In all its forms – as a tea, a tincture, its smoke, or simply as cut stems hanging over a bed or stashed under a pillow – mugwort can induce vivid dreams and help uncover, access and transform areas of psychic unconsciousness. This explains why the herb appears in many different myths, lore and literature across time. And dock? More than just a soothing balm for nettle stings, curled dock, for example, contains more vitamin C than oranges and more vitamin A than carrots.

Using 'weeds' in arrangements is not really a new concept for me. I've spent years exploring the properties of unwanted materials and questioning why they are so. I experiment with them. Do they stand up in water? What time in their cycle are they best picked? Where can I find them and when are they plentiful? What best to use for structure, texture, height, interest? But I still found working this arrangement incredibly difficult and challenging. No sooner had I started than there was fluff everywhere and I was battling with messy straggling stems, too much bulk and very few architectural elements. My idea of trying to force found stems into a preconceived design became a contradiction in terms. I saw the need to pause and rethink. Why was I trying to capture the wild, organic spread of weeds in a perfectly sculpted arrangement? What I really needed to do was give in to the plants and let them be. For, to see the beauty in the overlooked and unwanted is to see it as it really is.

Ingredients

Troughs measuring 15 x 15 x 10 cm
(6 x 6 x 4 in) x 2
Troughs measuring 30 x 11 x 5 cm
(12 x 4¹/₂ x 2in) x 2
Blocks of natural wool foam measuring
23 x 10 x 7.5 cm(9 x 4 x 3 in) x 3
(one cut in half)
Florist's pot tape
Strong scissors or secateurs
Moss x 2 buckets
Mugwort x 12 stems
Dock x 12 stems
Seedhead x 10 stems
Echinops x 30 stems
Heather x 5 small pots stems
Miscanthus grass x 20 stems
Blonde grass x 6 handfuls
Creeping thistle x 10 stems
Aster seedhead x 5 clumps
Quaking grass x 5 handfuls

Method

1. Line each trough with natural foam blocks and secure with waterproof tape. Using a jug or a watering can, pour water over the floral blocks until they start to sit in a little water.

2. Arrange the troughs in the rough shape of the arrangement you are creating – in my case, a wild meadowscape. Working with the troughs in situ allows you to keep a much better overview as the arrangement takes shape and you can develop the height and fullness of any given area.

3. Starting at the back, use the tallest stems to create the highest points. Rather than dotting the different stems around the arrangement, I tend to group them by variety – this is a much more realistic portrayal of the way a natural meadowscape grows.

4. Layer the ingredients in height order as you work towards the front of your display. As you do so keep an eye on the different tones of your stems. For example, in my arrangement, the grey echinops were not so visible set in front of the mugwort, so I put a layer of the blonde grasses in between them. Similarly, the rusty brown dock was lost against my exposed brick wall backdrop, so I layered it next to the rambling thistle in order for it to be seen.

5. As you approach the ground at the front section of the landscape, drape moss over the edges of the troughs and onto the ground, giving the appearance that the vegetation has simply sprouted there.

ABUNDANT STILL LIFE

*'Stop acting so small.
You are the universe
in ecstatic motion.'*

RUMI

*Brimming with a wealth of midsummer blooms
– hydrangeas, roses, rudbeckias – and with a
spattering of windfall fruit, this arrangement is a
fitting celebration of the sheer abundance of the
late summer months.*

Summer is the season of abundance and of gratitude. For me, as we head
into harvest, the weeks are filled with snippets from little yellow *Come and
Praise* songbooks, giving thanks for nature's gifts. This is a time of gathering
berries from hedgerows and apples from the lawn, of pick-your-own
strawberries (one straight in the mouth, one in the punnet and suspiciously
juicy red-stained smiles at the checkout). The Earth is literally gifting.

I have felt the strangest complications over this wealth of abundance:
it won't last, I don't deserve it, I can't pay it back. This is the voice that stands
on the shoulders of the deep feeler that perks up when something is pure
and wonderful. It was not until I delved into the mysterious world of
philosopher Alan Watts that my perspective began to shift and I started to
embrace the concept that as an apple tree 'apples', the Earth must 'people'.
We are the very fruit of the planet, and after all, the apple tree doesn't grow
its best apples out of shame or lack, but out of its abundance.

This perception of our place in the universe simultaneously erases our
sense of isolation and separateness as individuals and honours us
collectively as pioneers of cosmic phenomena. In the modern world, we are
frequently taught to see ourselves as individuals that came into this universe,
each unique and trapped within it. But what if, instead, we turn the concept
of our origin around and, for just one day, consider ourselves not to be single
characters on the Earth stage. Instead of viewing ourselves as strangers,
disconnected from nature, accept that we emerged from the universe. Just as
apples swell out of an apple tree or as a peony sprouts out of dirt into its
fullness, so too were you birthed from a long line of ancestors, one after
another. Not misplaced or detached, but with tangible links to way back in
time; a beautiful reflection of everything that is now and has come before.
In this way, collectively, we are abundance.

I find that from this place the guilt or notion of taking dissipates into
reciprocity. Gratitude sits side by side with what I can give back.

3

5

Ingredients

Large ceramic pitcher measuring
    35 x 15 cm (14 x 6 in)
Chicken wire measuring 40 x 40 cm
    (16 x 16 in)
Wire cutters
Gardening gloves
Florist's pot tape
Strong scissors or secateurs
Crab apple x 4 branches
Hydrangea paniculata x 2 stems
Dahlia 'Café au Lait' x 8 stems
Smoke bush x 2 stems
Garden rose x 5 stems
Phlox x 6 stems
Zinnia x 5 stems
Japanese anemone x 3 stems
Nasturtium x 3 vines
Rudbeckia x 5 stems
Snowberry x 2 stems
Windfall fruit

Method

1. Loosely scrunch up the chicken wire and place it inside the pitcher. Secure it by stretching a few strips of florist's pot tape across the top of the pitcher (see page 184). Fill the jug up to the brim with water, so that even the shortest stems will be able to drink.
2. Start to anchor your arrangement using the fullest or heaviest stems. In my display, I used the crab apple branches, the hydrangea paniculata, and the 'Café au Lait' dahlias as the sturdy foundation of my design.
3. With your foundational stems in situ, begin to build on the highest and lowest points of your arrangement. I found a delicate snowberry stem for my highest point, and started to fill out the spaces around the rim of the vase.
4. Use the fuller roses and dahlias to plug gaps between your anchor points, tucking some of them further back, while allowing others to burst out of the arrangement.
5. Pepper the phlox, small zinnias and Japanese anemones throughout the design and place the nasturtium vines so that they spill out over the edge of the vase.
6. Lastly, set the scene with windfall fruit, candles and any other little critters from the garden.

HEATHER FEAST GATHERING

*In this arrangement, blooms that are bold in
both form and colour take centre stage on a table
set for feasting out of doors, on moors dressed in
a carpet of heather.*

A dusky painted land. The air heavy with pollen. For just one month of the
year my neighbouring moorlands and hilltops are saturated in wild murky
purples, pinks and browns. There is a magic to this time of year – summer
going out with a bang – and there is a feeling that cannot be named, a potent
concoction of anticipation, wonder, grief.

It is no exaggeration to say that I dreamed this scene in my sleeping.
Of sitting awhile in some lavish celebration of the land's offering. A
gathering of friends, creating together and experiencing nature in among
the most exquisite of settings. Being together, to share, to laugh. Sharing
food, wine, stories . . . and watching as moths took the place of butterflies
with the setting sun.

It was in a small flatish clearing in the heather that we set this
arrangement, framed by a silver birch forest on one side and one of the many
dramatic cliff edges of the Peak District on the other. With just a few wooden
crates and planks of wood, we created a makeshift table for feasting, and
with it found an environment of wonder. When we make the effort to break
out of the comfortable, familiar patterns and do something different just
because, we make space for the extraordinary, whether that be found in a
conversation, a joke shared, a swarm of fireflies, a shooting star or a
candyfloss sunset. The seemingly small trinkets of beauty are always there
and available no matter what junk we consume with our minds. Let's make
hay while the sun shines, throw caution to the wind and dine among the
heather with friends.

Ingredients

Wooden crates and planks of wood
Table cloth
Cushions
Bowls for table centres,
    15 x 10 cm (6 x 4 in) x 4
Chicken wire measuring
    30 x 30 cm (12 x 12 in) x 4
Wire cutters
Gardening gloves
Florist's pot tape
Strong scissors or secateurs
Candlesticks
Candles

Flowers per arrangement:

Artichoke x 1 stem
Wax flower x 6 stems
Rudbeckia 'Sahara' x 3 stems
Anemone × hybrida *'September*
    Charm' x 3 stems
Rose 'Golden Mustard' x 3 stems
Echinacea x 6 stems
Smoke bush x 5 stems

Method

1. For each arrangement, scrunch the chicken wire into a loose ball and fit into one of the bowls. Stretch some strips of florist's pot tape across the top to stop the wire escaping (see page 184). Fill each bowl with water.

2. These arrangements have no foliage as such, so it is a question of packing them tight with flowers. The big heavy artichoke is best placed sitting at the base of the design, just resting on top of the rim of the bowl. This will weigh the whole arrangement down and keep it steady.

3. In order to balance out the artichoke, place the large-headed roses fairly low on the opposite side of the arrangement. Before placing them, use wax flowers to cover the chicken wire here, and to act as a backdrop for the roses.

4. You will still have around one third of the display to fill with the remaining flowers. Use puffs of smoke bush to cover any visible chicken wire and allow a few taller stems to jut out of the design to bring in both height and asymmetry.

5. Set your table, place the bowls down the centre and scatter leaves, sprigs or fruits between the bowls.

6. Light candles.

7. Pour wine and enjoy!

Heather is one of the botanical emblems of Scotland and in the Gaelic
language is 'fraoch'. Its blooms and their nectar have long been used
for their flavour. Archaeologists have even found traces of a fermented
heather drink on a 3,000-year-old shard of pottery on the Inner
Hebridean Isle of Rum. Today, a fine ale is made from heather mixed
with hops, barley, ginger and bog myrtle. In the Highlands, a
botanical infusion of heather tops was taken to treat coughs and
soothe the nerves, and heather-infused ointments treated conditions
such as arthritis and rheumatism. Highlanders also made heather tea:
'moorland tea', made from heather flowers combined with the dried
leaves of bilberry, blackberry, thyme and wild strawberry, was a
favourite of poet Robert Burns.

AUTUMN

The golden hour is now day-long, and the spare hour has been given back.
I've been warned not to do emotional maths, for where this soft heart
        meets ordered mind there can be troubling confusion

Now the Bracken is on the turn
I have a notebook where I write
the shade from ten to one
Every time I pass.

You see? Autumn likes to count backwards
The slow decent to the ground
The days get crunchier, nine, eight, seven, sharper,
        as the numbers slowly slide down to the soil.
Six leaves left on the Birch
Are falling like degrees
The great unlearning
The deep returning
November fifth, the tawny owl began her hoot at four.
I watched as she flew over the fire, as we moved closer to its heat,
        as we burned the last three logs on the pile.

This morning the pond was iced over
And my achy animal body felt relief as I lowered into the black
        hole of silky thick water.
Two herons, separately attended and left
Disappointed I was not a fish.
At one, we said our goodbyes. I laid my notebook down and began
        the journey under. Not long before
I picked the richest copper Bracken you ever did see

Autumn is a time for slowing down, for gathering and storing. It is a season of lasts: the last warm days, the last flowers to bloom, the last leaves to fall.

AUTUMN MUSINGS

It is the kind of conversation that only happens at 8 am en route to school with a sprightly jumping bean of a 10-year-old with blue hair, crunching through the crisp leaves as the wild wind shakes the trees and the sky does autumn confetti. 'What does autumn teach us, Mum?' This kind of deeply philosophical question, shot right out of nowhere, is what I live for. I've prepared for this, man, this is totally my bag. For now, however, I throw it back at him, for this is an occasion for his original thought.

'Everything is Change'

There's a palpable shift at the start of this season. You could say this for all four of them, but I find it most so in autumn. You can sense the summer's energy being stored, its life-force moving towards the ground. Mulch, humus and fire, root and spice, a wood-smoke aroma mixes with decaying leaf and new school shoes. New terms, new rhythms, new relationships meet old growth, old stories, darker nights. A muse for artists, poets, punks and philosophers, this is a season of complexly beautiful paradoxes. We are faced with pain or pleasure, the big and the small, becoming and dying, yet, as the German-Swiss poet and novelist Hermann Hesse writes, they are all part of the 'same stream', and we must try to let them all sit together.

It is, in my opinion, a conflict of life in the Western world that we constantly find ourselves resisting the desire to fall into slowness and hibernation at this time of year. We are peddled stories of success, of productivity, of working, socializing and people-pleasing. Spring growth pushes into summer frivolity. But when a plant in the garden starts to die back in the autumn, shedding its leaves or becoming a crispy brown, we don't panic and try to keep it alive, we don't stick the leaves back on. There is a general acceptance that this is the way of things, this is the season. We cut back, tend to the ground, mulch to protect and feed. With sadness, acceptance, hope and trust we prepare the way for something new to emerge in its time. Shouldn't we apply these practices to ourselves, too?

A significant number of my struggles in life arise from clinging to things that must die. I do anything I can to avoid feeling the sadness that is part and parcel of the flow of the seasons. But Autumn has a guiding way to reach past the surface, to go deeper down beneath the earth, to the very roots of a tree. To lay down and welcome Mother Nature's embrace.

Collecting Curios

As an avid collector of things, natural curiosities, found items and thrifted tat, I always welcome October with open arms and empty pockets. This year we collected a whole barrelful of conkers. Passers-by would stop to help, unable not to smile at this completely nonsensical act. Nobody asked, 'What will you do with them?' 'What are they for?' There's an unspoken agreement that collecting conkers is good for the soul. This act of scrambling around in the leaves, the satisfying release of the shell as you gently lower your foot onto it, the otherworldly shiny smoothness of the mahogany nut against the finest ivory silk.

This is just one of many simple and beautiful rituals that we can create at this time of year, as a way of connecting to the season and to ourselves, allowing our animal body to embrace the changes and a slower pace. The simplest of things is to gather herbs such as rosemary or cedar and throw them one by one into a fire as an act of prayer, intention or remembrance. Or spend a hazy afternoon creating a nature table in the garden, or a shrine, as an act of gratitude and stillness. We can dig up roots to make medicinal teas, acknowledging how the energy is being transferred to us and embracing the nutrition that had been held below the surface. I like to take every opportunity to nestle in blankets and woolly jumpers, to light a campfire and roast chestnuts. As simple as they may sound, performing these small acts year on year can help to ground you and connect you to the rhythms of the natural world, as you become swept along in nature's flow.

Harvest Time

More than any other, autumn is the season for stocking up the storecupboard and drying out stems for the months to come. I fill every crevice of the house with hanging bunches of foliage and herbs: mugwort, limonium, hydrangea. I load jars with hedgerow jams, elderberry cordial and rosehip syrup and pile stone bowls full of treasures for wreaths: seedheads, pinecones and branches. Towards the end of the season is when the evergreens start to dominate. Where once they would have blended into the big green tapestry, they now take centre stage among the backdrop of skeletons and bones. I welcome the nostalgic scent of conifer from childhood days of playing hide and seek, the rusty brown bark hairs on the trunk entangled with my own. As a child, a conifer was planted on the day I was born. We were one, growing together. By the time I was seven it could conceal me, and was a giant at age ten. At this age I judged foliage for its ability to provide a good hide-and-seek spot, hunkering down with woodlouse and spider, my autumn friends. I'd take the dusty pine over the large beech hedge any day, a whole third of the year regarded completely useless. Now I'm quite the opposite, transient delicate foliages in coppers and rusts; sun-bleached dried-out leaves that will fall at any minute, these are my choice leaves for arrangements in autumn.

And the flowers? Autumn flowers resemble a delicious pick-and-mix sweetshop of dahlias and zinnias, rudbeckia and helianthus. These are all certain kinds of rounded flowers in the shades of earth, sunrise, sunset, sand, turning leaf, clay and terracotta. Pompoms of flowers in a variety of sizes, perfect for crafting picture scapes of the season. I love to explore one hue right across the spectrum, found in foliage, flower, seedhead, container – earth tones and materials. For me, this represents everything returning back to the ground: clay, terracotta, petals, overripe berries, leaves and mulch.

Then comes the unconscious mental preparation for winter arranging, wreaths and garlands. Pine, spruce, cedar and juniper clear my mind, a palette cleanser . . .

AUTUMN

COLLECTION

AUTUMN PICK 'N' MIX

'I know of a bare attic-like room where one small vase of gay flowers makes it look furnished and decorated.'

CONSTANCE SPRY

Assembled in a derelict shop whose once-handsome decor is now faded and peeling, this eclectic fruity cocktail reflects on the passing of time as summer gives way to autumn. It is a celebration of the inevitable cycle of life.

Ever since they ripped out all the furnishings in the old kitchen shop across the street, I have admired its bare bones when walking past. Here is year upon year of wallpaper, where each layer has made a new fashion statement and provided the backdrop to a creative project, an inspiring display.

With the shop standing empty, I have watched the sunlight move across the road, from our flower shop in the morning, gradually becoming more and more golden before hitting this desolated space late in the afternoon. I'd wonder what flowers would suit the eclectic space, my imagination on fire.

It is remarkable just how many times I dream up a shoot or a project, build it up in my mind as some fantasy scenario only for it to take just a few conversations before I am there and it has become reality. Interactions with neighbours, business owners, parents at the school gate, interwoven, a web of connections. The spirit of neighbourly generosity is often much stronger than I imagine it to be – more so, I think, because of events in recent years. During the pandemic, the more restricted we became in our movement, the more confident I became at asking locally for what I needed. Lilac from a neighbouring garden, peonies from down the road. Writing and swapping notes posted through letterboxes, repaying favours with wreaths or bunches of homegrown tulips.

And that is how this kitchen shop arrangement came to fruition – in the simplest manner. It is a sweet shop pick 'n' mix of rudbeckia, dahlia and strawflower, little round blobs of colour against the vertical stripes of floral pattern and decoupage.

Ingredients

Terracotta bowl measuring
    15 x 15 cm (6 x 6 in)
Chicken wire measuring
    30 x 30 cm (12 x 12 in)
Wire cutters
Gardening gloves
Florist's pot tape
Strong scissors or secateurs
Viburnum foliage x 6 stems
Dahlia x 10 stems
Rose x 3 stems
Rudbeckia x 8 stems
Echinacea seedhead x 5 stems
Rosehip x 4 stems
Strawflower x 7 stems

Method

1. Scrunch the chicken wire into a loose ball that fits snugly inside your bowl. Secure across the top with a criss-cross of florist's tape (see page 184). Fill the bowl with water.
2. Begin by adding the foliage. To start with, use the autumn viburnum with berries to establish the overall shape of your arrangement. In my case, none of the stems were particularly long, so I just distributed them evenly throughout the bowl.
3. With the shape determined, use your largest blooms, the dahlias and the roses, to create anchor points in the design: the highest point, the widest point, some off-centre near the rim of the vase and the lowest dangling over the edge of the vase.
4. Now add the medium-sized flowers – the rudbeckia and echinacea seedheads – sticking a few in closer to the chicken wire and 'layering' others on top, bursting out of the design. Doing this creates depth and ensures nothing looks too flat.
5. Finally, dot the most delicate stems wherever a space needs filling or a line needs breaking up. The rosehips and strawflowers fulfil this brief perfectly.

4

NATURE'S TABLE

A demonstration of how nothing original or true, nor anything that holds meaning, can flow creatively without first being small and insignificant. In this project, curiosity follows where first the mind is still and has no intention.

'You must walk sometimes perfectly free, not prying or inquisitive, not bent on seeing things. [. . .] You must walk so gently as to hear the finest sounds, the faculties being in repose. Nature will bear the closest inspection. She invites us to lay our eye level with her smallest leaf, and take an insect view of its plain.'

HENRY DAVID THOREAU

When I did my art foundation course, a year's prelude to the university degree, I spent at least the first six or seven months grumbling about wanting to do some serious art, to be tutored in painting, in photography. Instead, what seemed to be happening was a series of daft exercises and gimmicks. When I expected to be thinking profoundly or desperately attaching some very obscure theory to a challenge, it would appear very forced and contrived. I was tearing my hair out!

Sitting and writing about creating this nature table reminded me of the kinds of projects we were being tasked with. 'Primary school nonsense', I would think to myself. 'I want to learn how to arrange flowers, not position scrap from a walk'. Yet I now know that the skill here is not in the arranging, the concepts, the clever colour palettes. No, the task is to let go of all that. This is about quietly observing, about feeling the textures of each little being. Here, as I run my finger across the smooth lining of a conker shell, I hum the familiar childhood song 'autumn days when the grass is jewelled and the silk inside a chestnut shell'. The moment expands; these silly tasks seem to create a space.

Much of the pleasure to be had from creating a nature table lies in collecting your 'specimens'. Choose a crisp, cloudless day to go hunting for twigs, pinecones, berries, fading blooms, conkers and newly fallen autumn leaves. Even before you start arranging, you will be exploring colour, texture and form.

Besides being good, all-round fun, conkers are rich little seeds full of interesting substances that include aescin, saponin and triterpenoids. Aescin is an anti-inflammatory that can help with bruises, sprains and other minor ailments. Many over-the-counter medicines for these conditions contain aescin. Placing a few conkers in the pockets of clothing hanging in wardrobes will deter moths! As the conkers dry out, they release triterpenoids into the air and moths are not at all fond of this chemical. The Vikings used conkers as a soap. The saponins found in conkers are naturally occurring plant glycosides (phytochemicals). They foam when mixed with water and have excellent detergent qualities.

Ingredients

A table, a board, some paper or the floor
Strong scissors or secateurs
Collection of autumn treasure

Method

1. Identify your space, the perimeter within which you want to work, and simply arrange your treasure.
2. Work with your finds as you decide where to place them in your arrangement. Break large stems down into smaller pieces, open some nutshells.
3. Explore each item and the different ways in which it can be displayed. This may include pulling apart petals or pressing flowers so they lie flat.
4. Feel the textures and observe the properties of everything as you piece the collection together on your surface.
5. Explore the relationships between different items, spiky and fragile, long tendrils and solid forms.

WITHERED

*This arrangement of scraps and 'past-it' blooms
signals one last heroic hurrah for the things
much loved but about to be lost.*

'*And all the lives we ever
lived and all the lives
to be are full of trees
and changing leaves.*'

VIRGINIA WOOLF

Once autumn is well underway, I start repeating the same mantra to myself, that this season is showing me how beautiful it is to let things go. I have to have it on repeat because it can feel so very hard.

With my thinking mind, I know that Mother Nature tells the glorious maple tree that it is time to shed its leaves and it does so in preparation for the winter ahead, to preserve energy. Only because of this deep underground nourishing is it then able to give forth the sap that gives us maple syrup. As far as I'm aware there is no bargaining that it needs the leaves for the photosynthesis that keeps it alive.

When a job does not work out, when a relationship ends or if we find ourselves in poor health, the part of us that is most closely linked to it – that has made that job or friendship part of us, this stubborn and desperate thread that is now causing us harm or pain – we have to let it go. It can be scary; it may mean freefalling, it may mean flying. Our human lives are full of cycles, possibly even more than those of nature. We travel through chapters in our emotions, spirituality and skill sets. Our tales twist and turn and the plot is messy and beautiful with complex simplicity. When 13th-century Persian poet Rumi talks about uncomfortable feelings, he suggests we welcome them in as they clear the furniture, ready for the new, for something wonderful.

This arrangement uses the scraps and 'past-it' blooms of late summer and early autumn. Working with flowers and foliage at this stage of life gives you the chance to feel their shift in energy and to observe the emotions that rise in you as you acknowledge the changes in their properties: the crisp surfaces of the leaves, the sour aroma of rotting berries, finding the perfect position for a rose and then watching as it suddenly decides to shed all its petals in one fell swoop. Compost-heap art.

5

Ingredients

Concrete trough measuring
 40 x 10 x 10 cm (16 x 4 x 4 in)
Chicken wire measuring
 40 x 25 cm (16 x 10 in)
Wire cutters
Gardening gloves
Moss x 4 handfuls
Florist's pot tape
Secateurs or strong scissors
Hawthorn x 3 branches
Snowberry x 5 stems
Privet x 10 stems
Nipplewort seedhead x 10 stems
Astrantia x 7 stems
Achillea x 5 stems
Crocosmia x 7 stems
Daucus x 5 stems
Bracken x 4 leaves
Rosehip x 3 stems
Jasmine x 6 stems
Rose x 14 stems

Method

1. Loosely scrunch the chicken wire into a snake that sits snugly inside the trough. Given that this is a relatively shallow container, stuff some moss in around the sides and crevices to stop water sloshing around.
2. Tape across the top of the trough in roughly three to five places to secure. Fill the trough with water.
3. This arrangement uses short stems on the whole. Place the foliage and seedheads first, distributing the stems and branches evenly along the length of the trough. Keep the height of this first 'layer' low and more or less even, with just a few taller stems to help create an organic, garden-style shape.
4. With the basic shape of the arrangement established, add all of the remaining leaves, berries and flowers, except the roses. Pepper the achillea, crocosmia and daucus the length of the design, interspersed with the bracken, rosehips and jasmine.
5. Once you are happy that the coverage and shape of the design is ready, carefully add the roses.
6. Dot them throughout the foliage and in clusters to give a natural 'as in the garden' look.
7. Allow some of them to droop over the edge of the trough with others placed higher up where their form can really be seen.

FRUITING STILL LIFE

*A two-fold project in which berries take centre
stage: a still-life arrangement that brings the best
of autumn's berries indoors and an elderberry
syrup to stir into hot drinks for fireside supping
in the night garden.*

A rich, earthy scent like no other hangs in the air in autumn, an aroma laced
with overtones of ripe and rotten, mulch and damp. This is a season for
slowing, gathering and storing. A season of lasts: the last dahlias, the last
chrysanthemums, the last leaf to fall. And what is left exposed and revealed
to all? The jewel-like orbs of elderberry, hawthorn and rosehip, fiercely
guarded behind sharp gnarly thorn protectors. Tiny birds dart between in a
dangerous dance.

Berries give themselves for plumping, nourishing and feeding the local
beings. Packed full of vitamins, antioxidants and flavonoids, they present
themselves as a medicine for the winter months ahead – Mother Nature
providing for her wild children.

I have never regretted taking the opportunity to make and store with
hedgerow treasures. There are few greater pleasures than sitting fireside in
December drinking a hot spiced elderberry cordial, held in the warm
embrace of the season's abundance. With the not-so-edible berries,
I arrange, complete with branch and withered leaf and the last blooms in
the garden. Privet, viburnum and amelanchier gently holding the rose,
dahlia and chrysanthemum. Meanwhile elderberries, rosehips, sloes and
hawthorn berries find their way into syrups and jams. I enjoy both practices
equally; one mainly nourishes my creativity and one mainly my body – both,
however, feed the soul.

2

Ingredients

Vase measuring 30 x 13 cm (12 x 5 in)
Chicken wire measuring
   30 x 30 cm (12 x 12 in)
Wire cutters
Gardening gloves
Florist's pot tape
Secateurs or strong scissors
Viburnum x 4 branches
Hawthorn x 3 branches
Privet x 5 branches
Pressed bracken x 6 leaves
Dahlia x 7 stems
Chrysanthemum x 5 stems
Rose x 3 stems
Crocosmia x 5 stems

Method

1. Loosely scrunch the chicken wire into a shape that fits inside your vase and stretch a few strips of tape across the top, creating a grid into which you can insert your stems (see page 184). Fill the vase with water.
2. Choose a couple of sculptural stems to establish the bare bones of your design. I chose an elegant branch of viburnum loaded with berries.
3. Add a few of the sturdier hawthorn and privet branches next, haphazardly crossing them to create a framework to support the less sturdy stems. Use these and the bracken leaves to set the overall shape of your design by creating its highest and widest points.
4. Place the largest focal blooms next, following the marker points that you have set with the foliage.
5. Add a few off-centre blooms in the middle area, too.
6. Make sure you have some of the foliage hanging over the sides of the vase here and there.
7. Intersperse the design with the smaller dahlias and the crocosmia, placing them between the larger blooms.

For elderberry syrup

Medium saucepan
Muslin cloth
Large bowl
Bottles
Water x 4 cups
Elderberries x 1.5 cups
Cinnamon x 3 sticks
Cloves x 1 tablespoonful
Sugar or raw honey x 1 cup

Method: Elderberry

1. Pour the water into a medium saucepan and add the elderberries, cinnamon and cloves.
2. Bring to a boil, cover and reduce the heat. Simmer for about 45 minutes to 1 hour, until the liquid has reduced by almost half.
3. Remove from the heat and leave until it is cool enough to handle. You can leave it overnight to steep.
4. Strain the liquid through a muslin cloth and into a bowl, discarding the elderberry mush.
5. Return the liquid to the pan and add the sugar or honey. Gently heat to dissolve.
6. Pour the syrup into a mason jar or glass bottle with a lid.
7. Store in the fridge and take daily for its immune-boosting properties. As with any herbal medicine, check with a health professional before taking regularly.
8. Mix a few spoonfuls with boiling water for a warming winter drink.

THE LAST CHRYSANTHEMUM

In this large, showy display, 'Vienna Copper' chrysanthemums emerge from an explosion of oranges, reds and yellows. It marks the most fitting finale for the season's blooms.

Having a background in art training and with an interest in Japanese prints, I had always considered the chrysanthemum a wonderous spectacle and found it strange to see it used formally in flower arranging. For a while, I completely lost interest in the bloom, separating that which I had seen and loved in the art world from that which you find in bright, plastic-wrapped bunches in supermarkets.

But with the resurgence of natural floristry, garden flowers and a wilder ethos to creativity in full swing, the creature-like chrysanthemum has shuffled its way back into my heart, along with haikus, poetry, paintings and symbolism. What other flower has had such a significant impact on global culture and literature? From ancient China to early Japan to England in the 1900s, 'mums' appear in the art of each area. It might be because of the flower's unique growth cycle and its ability to bloom later in the year. Or perhaps its popularity was founded in its medicinal properties, traditionally being regarded as a longevity tonic for general well-being – a soother of inflamed throats, a clearer of lungs, a reducer of fevers, and a digestive for bloating and cramping.

One thing I love about chrysanthemums as herbs is their dual-purpose as a moistener and as an astringent – such a rare pairing for one plant. This cooling, soothing flower is packed full of fortifying, tissue-protecting nutrients, antimicrobial constituents. It has a calming effect on the nervous system and can gently open the heart in its support of cardiovascular health. Have you ever inhaled the scent of a freshly cut chrysanthemum stem? It is one of my favourite aromas, a woody balm to the senses.

In this arrangement, I've assembled the very last flowers of the season in one blush, honey-toned elixir of blooms. The scale had to be big to allow the 'Vienna Copper' chrysanthemums the space and proportions to hold their own amid all the smaller spheres of sunshine.

*'Why should this flower
   delay so long
To show its
   tremulous plumes?
Now is the time of
   plaintive robin-song,
When flowers are
   in their tombs.*

*Through the slow
   summer, when the sun
Called to each
   frond and whorl
That all he could for
   flowers was being done,
Why did it not uncurl?'*

THOMAS HARDY

Ingredients

Antique iron urn measuring
  60 x 30 cm (24 x 12 in)*
Chicken wire measuring
  75 x 50 cm (30 x 20 in)
Wire cutters
Gardening gloves
Florist's pot tape
Secateurs or strong scissors
Beech x 5 branches
Viburnum x 8 branches
Elder x 4 branches
Rudbeckia 'Sahara' x 10 stems
Rose 'Notre Dame' x 8 stems
Rose 'Amnesia' x 8 stems
Rose 'Pride and Prejudice' x 8 stems
Chrysanthemum 'Vienna
  Copper' x 7 stems
Strawflower x 7 stems
Zinnia x 5 stems
Anemones x 5 stems

Method

1. Loosely scrunch the chicken wire and place inside your vessel. Secure a criss-cross of tape over the top to keep it in place (see page 184). Fill the urn with water.
2. Place the first few large branches of foliage – beech, viburnum and elder. As the end of the season approaches, each of these will have taken on its autumnal tones: copper for the beech, green through deep red for the viburnum, and a bleached-out look for the elder.
3. Use three striking roses to mark the highest and widest points in the arrangement. Then place the majority of your largest statement blooms – the chrysanthemums.
4. Dot the medium-sized blooms, the remaining roses and rudbeckia among the larger ones, taking care not to have them all at the same level. Tuck some of them right into the heart of the design and others protruding out.
5. Lastly, use the smallest flowers to act as a light seasoning, peppering strawflowers, zinnia and anemones throughout the design. Pay attention to any areas that look a little two-dimensional and allow these smaller flowers to jut out in places.

ALL
HALLOWS

*This huge sun wheel fashioned from honesty and
old man's beard serves as a portal from one
season to the next as autumn finally draws
to a close.*

In the northern hemisphere, Halloween is inextricably linked with autumn
and revolves around dressing up, carving decorations and trick-or-treating
through the streets. I face an annual internal battle wanting to champion
creativity, nature, crafting and storytelling while avoiding the crazily
consumerist consumption that goes with it. In wrestling back and forth,
what I have noticed is that what really ignites the kids' enthusiasm for this
time of year are the hours spent together making and the extra-weird and
wonderful conjuring up of the bizarre. When children work together on a
project, nothing is too crazy or too big to dream up. These activities trump a
fast plastic culture in every way and increasingly allow ancient legends to
creep back in, the telling of tales where the veil grows thin between the
world of form and the spirit world.

As nature begins to slow down, leaves fall and their energy is absorbed
inwards deep into the earth, my dreams take new shapes of being held
underground, furled in a fox set or burrow. I love to embrace the cold change
in season, welcoming its pace and solitude. And so to the more spiritual
celebration at this time of year, Samhain, a pagan festival originating from
an ancient Celtic tradition that welcomes in the harvest and ushers in 'the
dark half of the year'. Celebrants believe barriers between the physical world
and the spirit world break down during this time, allowing more interaction
between humans and dwellers of the otherworld. Once the harvest work
was complete, revellers joined with druid priests to light a community fire
using a wheel that would cause friction and spark flames. The wheel was
considered a representation of the sun, a symbol of gratitude and prayer.

This large-scale wreath is my take on a Samhain sun wheel and serves
as a portal between worlds. It is made with lunaria (honesty) and old man's
beard. Of witches and warlocks, it is a celebration of the turning seasons
and all that mystifies and carries us through the winter.

Ingredients

*Large wreath ring**
Secateurs or strong scissors
Twine or binding wire
Lunaria x 50 stems
Old man's beard x 30 vines measuring
1 m (3 ft) long

* *My wreath ring was purpose-forged from steel. You could equally successfully use a wreath made from willow or wood. Because the materials are all dried before assembly, there is no need to use any moss or covering for the frame.*

Method

1. To start, tie the binding wire to the frame using a firm knot – it needs to stay attached for the entirety of the wreath-making process.
2. Taking four of five mixed stems of lunaria and old man's beard, hold them together in a small bunch. I have cut some of my vines down into shorter lengths, while leaving others long to wrap around the wreath and give a more organic look.
3. Lay the bunch flat onto the ring, close to the tied-on wire. Wrap the bottom 2 cm (1 in) of the stems onto the frame, winding four or five times with the wire to secure it.
4. Now the process of layering your bunches around the circle can begin. Place the next bunch next to, but a few centimetres down from, the first, so that it covers the stems of the previous bundle.
5. Repeat this pattern as you move down and around the wreath, always covering the stems of the last bunch with the heads of the next.
6. As you reach your starting point – the first bunch – tuck the last few stems beneath its head.
7. Once the last bunch is secure, wrap the wire around a few extra times and snip it off.

WINTER

The novelty of light,
short, silvery and cold.
Numb fingers and aching bones,
familiar tingling skin as the blood slowly returns.
Bold colours that long to be seen,
the bluest sky,
the reddest berries,
whitest snow
and black bare earth.
The sharpest contrasts to keep us alert,
whispering quietly, don't forget the world outside.
Now all that is lost is renewing.
And that which is bare has roots growing.

This is the season of slowing, searching, paying attention and looking deeper.

WINTER MUSINGS

The winter season is for slowing and gathering. It is a time of reflection. I can so easily slip into the mentality, after Christmas, of longing and waiting for spring. Looking to the next, warmer, greener season. If we spend too much of our thought and energy pining for something else, we can too easily miss what is happening right in front of us at any given time. I am guilty of this. As soon as the new year begins, I am watching for new shoots, always checking the weather. I am eating my breakfast whilst mentally planning my lunch, so to say. Meanwhile, outside, nature is working miracles. Frost and ice encase leaves into pieces of art. Flowers are blooming in sheltered, quiet places and bright rich berries are popping with colour in a land that is awash with white and grey.

Winter Flowers

The persistent, resilient strength required for a plant to grow and bloom through the harshest of winter weather is something I find profoundly beautiful. Gathering the season's few flowers and bringing them into the warmth and heart of the home can be a mindful practice of living fully in the season. In winter, fruiting branches, berries and fungi become exciting ingredients to intersperse with available blooms. They all add to the scene and bring into the home some of nature's wonders, quieter and more curious counterparts to showy dramatic flowers that often take centre stage.

Arranging with natural products in the colder seasons has its challenges, some more physical than others. Snow, frost and ice can literally prevent us from venturing too far from home and bringing in even the most minimal ingredients to work with. This provides an opportunity to be fiercely creative, to find abundance in scarcity, beauty in the mundane. Creating a winter arrangement can be as simple as hanging a single, twisted bough on the wall or filling a vase with red-berried twigs. Here, the smallest, quietest nod to what is happening in winter can help to connect us with the season and move with its rhythms.

Flower-arranging can become a truly contemplative practice. Take the time to consider each stem for its unique characteristics – its curves and bends. Assess the weight of a heavy bloom or the twists of a gnarly branch. To understand each flower's form and movement is to know where to place it in a design for it to be seen and enjoyed at its best. Every year, I forget how to use a stem of amaryllis in a bouquet or arrangement. Its big, heavy bloom faces downwards, its hollow stem large and fragile. Working with it again is like greeting an old friend and having a catch-up, remembering particular quirks and characteristics.

Open-Air Living

There can be so little motivation to go outside in the colder months, but we should take our lead from our Scandinavian neighbours who approach winter as a special time of year bursting with opportunities for enjoyment and fulfilment. As Aristotle reminds us: 'To appreciate the beauty of a snowflake it is necessary to stand out in the cold'. The Norwegians embrace the concept of *friluftsliv* (open-air living), which was popularized in the 1850s by the playwright and poet Henrik Ibsen. The term describes the importance of spending time outside, in nature, for both spiritual and physical wellbeing. Combine this with the Danish principles of *hygge* (comfort, warmth and slow contentment) and there's a beautiful pattern of being outdoors with nature, slowing down, being in the moment, observing self-care, ritual and quietude.

A true winter pleasure for me is to pursue my love for wild swimming. Even its very title 'wild' suggests a loss of connection with the outdoors, for really it is just 'swimming'. I've forever been pulled to the water, lakes, rivers, the sea – even murky canals as a bored, rebellious teen. The rituals of calming the mind and entering the water, constantly listening to my body, respecting the water, the wild, leaving all ego at the shore. The almighty sensation as the cold knocks the air out of me, and all I can do in that moment is slowly . . . breathe. Crossing the border from one matter to another, the glacial water being a different realm. It has the power to completely shift perspective. Then comes the after swim, the rush, the endorphins and sense of oneness with all. The warming up, a hot flask of something with some spice. A comforting, nostalgic hot-water bottle. This, for me, is *friluftsliv*, this is *hygge*, and I'm in deep.

We Are Nature

Noticing the small things on winter walks can lead to great inspiration, so much so that I've made it a discipline no matter what the weather, to take a short break outside every day. It can do wonders for stirring creativity. Wintry light has its own hue, a bluish, cold yellow. I like to observe my breath as it turns to steam, exhaling with the suburban houses and steamy central heating, inhaling with the birds. There's wonder to be had from spotting different views of the landscape through the skeletons of naked trees or looking up to see the twists and coils of a majestic plane tree adorned with dangling seedhead baubles. Pausing to admire a tiny moss universe on a drystone wall encrusted with frost, my senses might catch the sweetness of a blooming viburnum or winter jasmine. Just imagine if I had missed this by rushing or indeed not venturing out at all.

I want to savour it all and to sing in gratitude to the winter, to thank her for sheltering those who are shy, for the quiet, still darkness that cocoons me, muting the mind's cacophony. Stepping out in winter, I am served the gentle reminder that I am not separate from the birds that flit and dance in the barren bushes. As I carve my step, I am aware of my heavy, cold breath, in and out of me, in and out of the starlings, in and out of the oak tree standing proud in bare bones, exposed. Our veins like root systems, our breath flowing in and out of each other. Gathering, collecting, observing, creating.

Ready for new growth. The same air, same essence, we are all made from star dust. We are nature.

WINTER

COLLECTION

MUSHROOM ALTAR

This flat lay explores the depth of connectedness, the magic and the scale of time that the mushroom kingdom weaves through this world, sustaining the lives of many.

Occasionally my attention is pulled, a fascination grows and my curiosity is sparked by a new thing that also somehow feels like an old longing or reconciliation with a passion that's been lost for years. Nothing has achieved this quite so profoundly as the complicated, beautiful and unknown world of mycelium.

Rewind 30-odd years and you would find me in a child-sized hole in the middle of the compost heap, a rat child having made a den among the rotting matter somewhere between death and rich newness. I would marvel at the things I found there, in quiet solitude where grown, clean, loud people never thought to look; singing gleefully, 'I am leaf, I am dirt, I am mushroom, I am Earth. I am bird and rodent, toad and woodlouse. I am rose, honeysuckle, bones and feathers. I am, I am.'

I have found that, once your eyes open just the tiniest fraction to these beautiful, mysterious, magical fruits, you begin to see them everywhere. It is as if a veil has been lifted and nothing makes sense anymore and equally there is astounding clarity. I'm no expert on anything, but what I lack in knowledge I make up for in enthusiasm. I go on mushroom walks with identification apps and books, taking the long route home to find the good spots – early morning wandering amid mists, suburban ghosts and birdsong. The pecking order of beings on this Earth begins to shift. The story that we humans are in charge is, as American poet Ralph Waldo Emerson would say, 'hobgoblin to little minds'.

This kind of flat lay involves a simple process of arranging specimens with spaces in between that form a shape. I always start in the centre and work my way outwards. The result, on this occasion, is an altar to that which I do not understand. It is all about seeking out the weird and wonderful in unexpected places, learning about poisons and healing properties, nutrition and toxicity. It is about keeping track of where things grow and what conditions are rife. Above all it is about recognizing that our species, in all its fast and vast knowledge and technology, is also so very small.

Ingredients

A textured board, table or floor
Varieties of fungi, lichen or moss

Method

1. Start by placing something very focal at the centre of your board. For me it was a somewhat faded and tattered fly agaric mushroom.
2. Place some more of the larger fungi around it, creating an overall look that is balanced.
3. In between the larger specimens, place the smaller, more delicate mushrooms. Consider their forms and intersperse those with long stalks with others that have interesting gills.
4. Add back any tiny bits of earth, twig and moss to fill small gaps and to contribute textures of a different kind.

MOORLAND CLOUD

'The colour of springtime is in the flowers; the colour of winter is in the imagination.'

TERRI GUILLEMETS

This cloudlike installation conjures the subtle shades of a winter sunrise. A hanging arrangement floating in space, an oddity in a room. This is not conventional, or what you might expect to see, yet it draws you in, makes you question, feels surreal.

In winter, flower art has the capacity to bend towards the extraordinary – not through the use of extravagant or exotic blooms, but via the narrative that the creator weaves within an arrangement. Here is an opportunity to make suggestions, to open up doors and use gentle signposts to encourage the viewer to look from within. For, in this season, the looking is necessary.

Memories and nostalgia can drive the energy of a design, keeping it vibrant and personal. This arrangement was inspired by a winter sunrise swim out in the moorlands of the Peak District. As the sun rose and the full moon set on the pale, frost-covered wild grasses and bracken, the hills became blushed with pale pink, the darkest tones a deep crimson. I suddenly saw an alien landscape born of dreams and imagination. This was the unlikeliest place for anything to bloom and thrive, a strange moonscape, and yet it reminded me of the several-century-old popular Greek folk song: 'Look at the amaranth: on tall mountains it grows, on the very stones and rocks and places inaccessible.' Amaranthus or love-lies-bleeding is one of my go-to flowers for suspended designs. Its cascading form literally drips from an installation, blurring the lines of the familiar, the unknown. People question, 'What is that?' 'Is it real?' Working with the horizontals and verticals of the natural world, here every stem plays a part in the sculpting of both the shape and tale we are telling.

In interviews, I am often asked what inspires my work. Where, once, I might have looked to other genres of art and design or fashion to answer this question, I now find it lies in fleeting observations of nature that feel like a sudden blow to the head. The experience, sight and depth of awe in seeing this moorland landscape scene burned on my retinas, leaving me with the sense that it was time to make. When an image haunts and colours the hours, days, and sometimes even dreams, there is very little else to do than express it creatively. This cloud was indeed an act of creative inspiration articulated through flowers.

Ingredients

Long, sturdy branch measuring
    1.5 m (5 ft)
Chicken wire measuring 2.5 m x 30 cm
    (8 ft x 12 in)
Wire cutters
Gardening gloves
String or cable ties
Cup hook or nail x 2
Strong scissors or secateurs
Different grasses x 4 bundles
Dried miscanthus grass x 30 stems
Dried limonium x 30 stems
Amaranthus x 40 stems

Method

1. Using the branch as the base support, create a chicken-wire structure for a suspended installation (see page 188). Wrap chicken wire around its entire length, scrunching it into the branch in places.
2. In some areas, sculpt the wire to create an overall shape that is more organic and asymmetrical rather than forming a straight tube that simply follows the line of the branch.
3. Use string or cable ties to secure the wire in three or four places along the length of the branch. At either end, tie a 2 m (6½ ft) length of string from which to suspend the form between two small hooks screwed into the wall, high up and out of sight.
4. Once the frame is hanging in situ, work from left to right to fill the wire with your dry ingredients. I placed a burst of grasses at the left end, all grouped together for a dramatic impact and stretching towards the light of the window. Work in groups rather than single stems, which would take a long time and create a lot of mess.
5. Towards the middle of the arrangement, start to blend in the fluffy miscanthus grass. I chose a blush shade. Reminiscent of the dawn moorland landscape, it subtly bridges the transition from the tones of the natural grasses to the pink of the limonium. As I continued to fill the chicken wire, I created a small dip in the shape of the design, near the middle. The aim is to keep an organic flow, to introduce an inconsistency that gives a more haphazard or asymmetrical look.
6. Not wanting to overwhelm the design with the brighter pink of the limonium, I used it in smaller quantities in the sparser middle section of the installation.
7. I kept the last third of the design, the end furthest from the window, for the amaranthus stems. Slightly more in shadow here, they play on the mystery and depth of the arrangement. I nestled some stems in close to the wire, to cover the mechanics of the design, and placed others jutting out further and higher up to really make use of their cascading effect.

3

4

6

7

LEARN TO LET GO

It is in winter that everlasting flowers, dried grasses and seedheads come into fruition. To work truly seasonally, these are a staple ingredient for any floral designer. They really come into their own used in temporary arrangements rather than being held on to forever, simply because you can or must. Nothing really lasts forever and these dried blooms, in my experience, are best enjoyed for a season before letting go and embracing new growth.

FROZEN
IN TIME

'Absolute attention
is prayer'

SIMONE WEIL

*A cloche arrangement – an act of bringing
attention to the small things. Assembling the
smallest scraps of the most curious winter
flowers under glass freezes a moment in time
and has the effect of magnifying the blooms.*

A cloche arrangement at this time of year can make a really unique
centrepiece for a special dinner or gathering. The magical nature of flowers
under glass combined with twinkling candlelight is evocative of a fairy-tale
scene from *Beauty and the Beast*. The arranging itself is simple. Anything
goes here: scraps of foliage from the garden, feathers, flowers and twigs. It is
a collector's dream, a cross between flower-arranging and a botanical
exploration.

When gathering for this cloche arrangement, I had to let go of an initial
desire for something more glamorous, more impressive. At any time of year,
but more so in winter, you cannot depend on certain flowers being available
when you want them. I had high hopes for exquisite, speckled hellebores,
heirloom snowdrops and slipper orchids. But nature's timing does not
always fit in with ours and we must be patient and adapt.

Patience is not just something we develop; it is a vitality we walk with,
our tread, slow and even, taking in all beauty, and waiting quietly. Patience
also holds unfathomable wisdom and deep experience. She says, 'Here,
watch the sunlight dance on this wall and see how those tiny intricate stems
produce the finest shadows. Here, see them magnified! Did you ever see
something as utterly magnificent as the first quince blossom? See the
abundance around you now! Not what could have been or what should have
been, but what is right now.' The practice of creating something so small, so
intricate, with just tiny, gathered bits and bobs holds such valuable lessons.
And so my arrangement took shape using what I had at first considered
scraps or plan B ingredients: devilishly thorny, twisted quince from an
overgrown urban car park, a single hellebore from the garden, some pressed
ferns that fell out of an old book from years past and a vine of winter-
flowering clematis. Not forgetting the crab apples that pop against the snow.
There's an alchemy that I cannot explain and do not fully understand, as if
nature knows best and wants to gently guide the design.

Ingredients

Small shallow dish measuring
5 x 10 cm (2 x 4 in)
Chicken wire measuring
30 x 30 cm (12 x 12 in)
Florist's pot tape
Strong scissors or secateurs
Glass cloche or bell jar
Quince blossom x 3 branches
Crab apple x 3 branches
Anemone x 3 stems
Hellebore x 2 stems
Narcissus x 3 stems
Winter clematis x 2 stems
Privet x 3 leaves
Small fern x 5 leaves
Pepper berry x 5 clusters

Method

1. Take a small shallow dish and place a scrunched ball of chicken wire inside, taping securely (see page 184). Add the tallest twigs and blooms first – in my case, a couple sprigs of quince blossom and crab apple.
2. Stagger the flower stems at different heights, adding a few statement anemones, hellebores and narcissi lower down for balance. Each time you add a stem, lower the glass dome in place to check size and proportion.
3. See if you can play with the flexibility in the tallest stems of winter clematis so that they bend and curve to the shape of the glass.
4. Lastly, fill out the base more densely with items that do not need water – feathers, ferns, pinecones, shells or fruit. Secure each into the base using wire, with the odd flowers and stems dotted among them.

SOLSTICE CROWN

Fashioned out of stems rescued from the old, the weathered and the fallen, this flower crown was created in celebration of the winter solstice, a time when the days start to grow longer once more.

'*May you grow still enough to hear the small noises earth makes in preparing for the long sleep of winter, so that you yourself may grow calm and grounded deep within.*'

BROTHER DAVID STEINDL-RAST

There are certain phenomena for each of us that act as a door or a bridge, or a border perhaps, from one realm to another. Have you ever stood in awe and felt a strange and wonderful longing just to melt into a view or painting? It could be a sunset or bird song, a particular piece of music or poem, a tree in full blossom or the smell of hot pavement after rain. Cold water is my door into stillness. Crossing from land into the unknown, there is no other feeling quite like it. There is always apprehension and a certain sense of danger. Midwinter brings opportunities to deepen my relationship with the cold, to experience and respect it to the utmost.

I was brought up in the Christian faith, with rituals such as communion, baptism, liturgies and prayer. Advent, Christmas, New Year. It's not that I reject them now, but I never really chose them for myself; it was just something we did without question or exploration. The idea that you could atone through resolutions based in shame sat uncomfortably with me. I did, however, feel fondly for the feelings of repetition, grounding and a sense of belonging, all of which helped me to form new rituals for myself, of my choosing, with which to honour and celebrate the divine, and to acknowledge growth and change.

Winter solstice signals the slow return of light and the celebration of all that is nurtured in darkness: seeds, mycelium, roots and earthworms; silent prayers, longings and fears; dried grasses and deadheads in the garden. This is a time for giving thanks for the shadows and the quiet, for the shy ones that work to fertilize and restore.

I made it with a vision of folklore white witches and selkies as a way of celebrating the magic of the season. This had a slower, more detailed and focused pace of arranging. Each fragile stem was placed one at a time, bound and set, layer upon layer. This became the mantra for the ritual. Taking the old fragile bones and laying them down, appreciating their part in the electricity of all things.

Ingredients

Headband
Small-gauge chicken wire measuring
    20 x 20 cm (8 x 8 in)
Short wire x 5
Hot-glue gun
Nipplewort seedhead x 5 stems
Mugwort x 2 stems
Bracken x 1 leaf
Lunaria x 4 stems
Strawflower x 10 stems
Pepper berry x 6 clusters

Method

1. Tightly scrunch the chicken wire into a single length that is around 3 cm (1¼ in) thick. Mould the wire to the shape of the headband and attach it into place with the single short wires – one at each end and three evenly spaced in between.
2. Start by placing the delicate nipplewort seedheads at the tallest points, sliding and pushing each stem into the wire until secure. Keep the stems at the centre of the headband slightly taller than those at either end.
3. Add the mid-length mugwort stems and individual fronds of bracken now – interspersing them between the seedheads.
4. Create a shorter layer using lunaria, mugwort and strawflowers. All of these flowers are super-delicate, so take time as you slot the stems into the wire. As you build up your layers, you will find that some stems are supported by the nest of materials already in place.
5. Finally, closest to the hairband, weave in some of the larger strawflowers and clusters of pepper berry (I attached my pepper berry stems to thin wire to help support them).
6. On the underside of the hairband – the part that will be closest to your head – use a glue gun to seal everything and to stop tiny stems slipping through.
7. If you would like the crown to be double-sided, repeat the steps in a simpler fashion on the other side.

GATHERED & WOVEN

'What did you do as a
child that made the
hours pass like minutes?
Herein lies the key to
your earthly pursuits.'

CARL JUNG

*This wreath conjures days of childhood,
of moments spent immersed in nature. Part
wreath, part nest; gathered, woven, smelled,
touched, it is an act of returning to the wild.*

There was a time when I spent days hiding in the woods, a member of a secret club with squirrels or making nests in cornfields or, better still, from freshly cut grass; a time when camping out in a warm putrid den carved out of the compost heap was marvellous and woodlice made for wonderous little discoveries under every upturned rock. I felt so connected. There was no separation between myself and the field mouse or the robin. I understood the wildflowers, the forbidden overgrown garden of shoulder-height dandelion clocks, the air dense with seeds. I could weave my way through beautiful transparent nettles, a dirty dancing dance, a deathly challenge.

This time came before a raging sea of expectations, negative self-beliefs and anxiety completely drenched me after just wading in for a quick dip. For, gradually, the bones I had collected on walks and meticulously scrubbed with washing-up liquid became embarrassing and I began to think that, perhaps, there was something wrong with me for believing I could rebuild the sheep. I stopped pursuing that very natural and free-spirited curiosity for life and death, for internal things, for depth and dirt.

Discovering the above quote by Carl Jung as an adult, I had a moment of illumination. This is for me! I had spent the majority of my adult life craving those simpler childhood times, longing to play and create freely, and I realized that I now satisfy this yearning through my work. I find joy and wonder in the woody scent of a freshly cut stem or the velvet touch of a petal. It is at times like this that I become immersed once again in nature.

For me, ancient tales passed down through generations add another layer of wonder to creating, often informing the stems I choose. In witchcraft, lunaria is considered protective, keeping away evil spirits and beasts. Rosebay willow herb grows in poor soil and has, in the past, been referred to as bombweed, as it would always be the first flower to grow on the land destroyed during wartime bombing. By winter, all that is left are skeletal bones, scrappy twisted stems with remnants of dried-up fluff add a wispy, nest-like texture that are perfect for wreaths and winter arrangements. And, so, here lies the inspiration for this project.

3

5

Ingredients

Wire or wicker/birch wreath frame
*   measuring 30 cm (12 in) in diameter*
Reel wire or string
Strong scissors or secateurs
Moss
Rosebay willowherb x 15 stems
Limonium x 20 stems
Euphorbia spinosa *x 5 stems*
Dried strawflower x 40 stems
Lunaria x 10 seedheads
Velvet ribbon measuring 1.5 m (5 ft)

Method

1. Attach the reel wire or string to the wreath frame by wrapping it around once or twice and tying a knot (see page 190). Keep this fixed to the wreath for the entirety of the making – you will continue to wrap the wire around the frame as you add your stems.
2. Start by adding small clumps of moss to the wreath, wrapping with wire to secure. Work your way around the entire frame in this way.
3. Now, follow the same pattern of moving around the frame, but this time with the foliage and branches. Lay small, hand-sized bunches flat on the wreath and wrap just the bottom 2 cm (1 in) of stem tightly to the frame.
4. Vary the stems a little in each bunch, and lay each one on top of the last, but staggered slightly to cover its stems.
5. Work your way around the wreath, alternating the positions of the bunches to face slightly towards the inner perimeter of the wreath and then the outer perimeter.
6. With the wreath complete, you can tie off or cut the wire. Finish with a ribbon, a favourite piece of fabric or nothing at all.

DANCE OF DUALITY

'What makes night within
us may leave stars.'

VICTOR HUGO

*A study of light and dark, this arrangement has
pale white anemones as its focus, offset with the
muted browns of eucalyptus, bracken and the
deep black berries of viburnum.*

On a cold, stark winter's day nothing feels more fitting than a vase full of
anemones with papery white and blush petals and their inky black centres
quietly fluttering, like the soft eyes of winter. These dramatic dark hearts
make it easy to pair these blooms with nearby-growing viburnum, steel
berry or privet. The faintest wash of a cold pink on some of the petals is
further accentuated by *eucalyptus stuartiana* and bracken.

   The first mention of the anemone flower in Western culture was in
ancient Greece. Its name comes from the Greek word *anemo*, which means
'wind'. Anemones arrive early in the year, just before the seasons change.
They seem to beckon spring in and, as a result, they have come to symbolize
an anticipatory air. The idea that anemones signify anticipation makes them
quite the appropriate New Year flower.

   What I find most comforting about an armful of anemones in full bloom
is their dance between soft and strong, light and dark, petal and fur. To hold
all dualities together and let them just be. To feel joy despite pain, to love and
let something go, to be nourished in the darkest moments and to grow
through decay.

   And so, I take a tiny step forward and I make – not for perfection or to
better myself. I make because the alternative is to not make and there are
plenty of other thrashing dragons that I'll need to be duelling this year for
this also to be locked up waiting for me on the sidelines. I find a surprising
comfort in the gentle simplicity of the many ruffles of petals and the warmth
of the leaves. I neither love nor loathe the result.

Ingredients

Ceramic pot measuring
    15 x 15 cm (6 x 6 in)
Chicken wire measuring
    30 x 30 cm (12 x 12 in)
Wire cutters
Gardening gloves
Florist's pot tape
Secateurs or strong scissors
Eucalyptus stuartiana *x 6 stems*
Eucalyptus populus *x 5 stems*
Steel berry *x 6 stems*
Bracken *x 4 leaves*
Anemone *x 12 stems*
Ranunculus *x 12 stems*
Waxflower *x 7 stems*

Method

1. Lightly scrunch the chicken wire into a ball that fits snugly inside your pot. Secure with a criss-cross of tape across the top (see page 184). Fill with water.
2. Begin a framework of foliage – eucalyptus, steel berry and bracken – to create a base into which the flowers will sit. Keep it fairly compact. The overall look you are aiming for is a blousy mass of white/blush flowers. Going too large at this point will mean everything has to be more spaced out.
3. Add the shortest and smallest blooms next, tucking them in close to the chicken wire, nestled among the foliage.
4. With the remaining larger flowers, leave their stems a little longer so that they jump out of the design at different levels.
5. Choose one particularly long stem for the tallest point of your design and another, more curved stem, to drape over the edge.
6. Add the waxflower stems in between the blooms to fill out any gaps or break up any solid lines.

FLORISTRY BASICS

A Florist's Toolkit

Most of the arrangements in this book can be made using a very basic toolkit. There may be a few additional items here and there – a plinth in Smoke & Grey (see pages 66–71) or a hot-glue gun for the Solstice Crown (see pages 160–163), for example. You will find these listed with the ingredients for each project.

Strong scissors

A good pair of strong scissors is essential for working with flowers. Buy a pair with carbon blades, if you can, as these can be sharpened and so the scissors should last a lifetime.

Secateurs

Regular garden secateurs are useful for cutting woody stems and large branches.

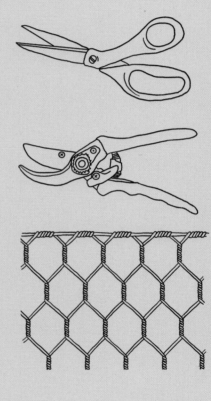

Chicken wire

Almost all of the projects in this book use chicken wire one way or another. A fine-mesh version is good for vase arrangements, as it is flexible and can be moulded into balls for placing inside bowls and vases for small arrangements. It also makes a good base for bigger displays. Use a more industrial-strength chicken wire for larger installations. You can buy it in hardware stores and garden centres.

Wreath wire

Flexible but strong wire is good for making wreaths and floral crowns for both indoor and outdoor use/wear. Expect to use almost a full roll per wreath.

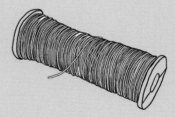

Wire cutters

Do not be tempted to use scissors for cutting chicken or wreath wire, as this can blunt them. A small pair of wire cutters is the better option.

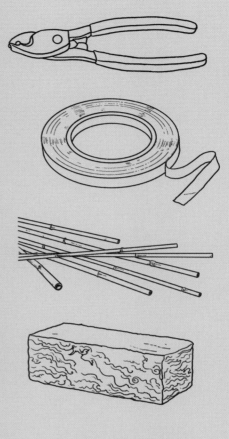

Florist's pot tape

Use this either to create a grid over the top of a vase or bowl (see page 183) or to secure chicken wire inside a vessel. It should have a strong adhesive and be waterproof.

Bamboo canes

Various lengths of bamboo canes can be useful for adding extra support to a tall arrangement or installation.

Natural floral blocks

These offer a green and sustainable alternative to floral foam, a single-use plastic that is harmful to the environment. Look for blocks made from wool foam or similar biodegradable and compostable natural materials.

Cable ties

Large installations using chicken wire sometimes require a sturdier, stronger method of attachment than florist's pot tape. Cable ties ensure a design is securely attached to its frame or hanging point.

Gardening gloves

Wear thick, protective gardening gloves when handling rough or spiky stems. You can also wear them when handling chicken wire, which can have sharp edges.

CHOOSING & BUYING FLOWERS

During the pandemic months, I grew accustomed, more than ever before, to using what was readily available: seasonal blooms and foliage, overgrown branches, fruits and vegetables. I know not everyone has access to a garden brimming with flowers year-round, but it is surprising how resourceful you can be and how arrangements can be bolstered with foliage, seedheads and 'weeds'.

Using what is available and in season not only minimizes the environmental impact on our planet, but also ensures you get blooms at their very best. It is also more cost-effective. If an arrangement is begging for a more tropical flower or a bloom that is out of season, ask your florist where it was grown and if it has come from a fair-trade farm. At Swallows and Damsons, we always enquire after the origins of our flowers. There is infinitely more pleasure in working with bunches of flowers and sprays that have been grown ethically.

When cutting from your own garden, the best times to harvest plants is either first thing in the morning or at dusk, as this is when the stems are turgid and full of water. Avoid cutting stems when it is very hot and sunny as they can be water-stressed and may wilt immediately with little chance of recovery. Always have a bucket of water close by and place freshly cut flowers into it immediately after cutting. Keep all flowers in water until you are ready to create an arrangement. Plants that are newly in bud may struggle to flower once cut, so wait until they are showing a little colour and signs of opening. The exceptions to this rule are hellebores and hydrangeas, both of which benefit from being left in the garden until they have bloomed for a while. Hellebores go to seed at this stage, forming a bulbous pod at the centre of the flower head. If cut at this point, they can last weeks. Similarly, hydrangea petals become stiffer and more paper like, and will often dry out perfectly, retaining their colour and lasting for years as dried flowers.

Any flowers available to buy in a flower shop should be at the correct stage for making arrangements of all kinds. Do not be afraid to ask for advice on how long certain buds will take to open or how long blooms will last in a vase once fully opened. At a farmers' market, you can talk directly to the suppliers about the methods they use to grow their plants and will always benefit from their knowledge.

PREPARING FLOWERS

It is sensible to carry out some advance preparation of your stems before arranging them, as this will allow them to really thrive in the design. It may be that you want all stems of a certain type to be the same height, for example, or for an arrangement to have less foliage. Not only that, but trimming stems ensures that they have the longest possible vase life.

Cutting Stems

As soon as a stem has been cut, its protective defence mechanism kicks in and it starts to seal in order to retain moisture. Immediately placing the stem in water can halt this process. Then, every time the stem is subsequently taken out of the water, no matter how long for, you should trim a small amount from the base before placing it back into water. Do this by cutting 1 cm ($^{1}/_{2}$ in) off the stem at an angle. This allows a greater surface area for the flower to drink up as much water as possible.

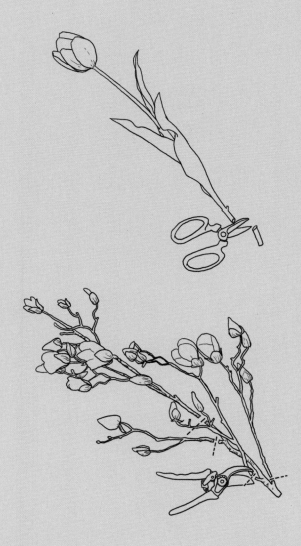

Large Branches

Depending on how you want to use a large branch or 'spray' stem with more than one flower head, you can divide it up into smaller blooms. As long as each stem can reach the water in a vase, there are no rules as to how many divisions you make.

Foliage

Foliage can make or break a design, depending on the overall look that you are going for. Certainly, below the water line, you should aim to have no foliage at all. This is because leaves rot when submerged in the water, and this increases bacteria and shortens the vase life of your flowers. You can remove any leaves from a stem using scissors or simply by snapping them off with your hand. It is also a good idea to snip off any large thorns from a stem that might be painful if accidentally grabbed when arranging.

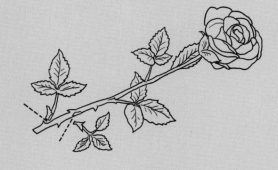

Searing Flowers

Revive flowers that appear floppy by plunging their stems into boiling-hot water before adding to a design. This forces air out of the stem and encourages a better uptake of water. To do this, fill a container with a little freshly boiled water and hold the cut stem in the water for around 30 seconds. Use your judgement here: a hard, woody stem may need longer, whereas a particularly soft, delicate stem will need less. Re-cut the stem end and rest it in fresh water overnight before using in an arrangement. If the stem is very short, carefully wrap the flower head in some paper before searing, as hot steam can scald delicate petals.

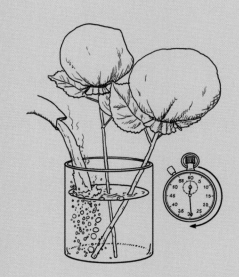

Extending Vase Life

While every variety of flower has a different vase life, there are a couple of ways to ensure that you get the most time to appreciate each arrangement.

- *Keep cool:* The cooler the temperature in a room, the longer the flowers will last. Be sure to keep an arrangement away from heat sources and out of direct sunlight.
- *Stay fresh:* Bacteria build-up in vases is a sure and smelly way to finish off flowers before their time. To keep water fresh, top it up whenever the level is low, or carefully pour water out and refresh with clean water after a few days.
- *Stay natural:* The process of flowers wilting and drying out can be incredibly beautiful and a ritual that is celebrated throughout the seasons. Once in a while, embrace an arrangement's natural decaying process, rather than being quick to discard as soon as the flowers look past their 'best'.

BASIC METHODS

When choosing the correct method for a floral arrangement, you need to think about the look you want to achieve in terms of size, height, vase and style of design, but also to bear in mind the space in which an arrangement will be situated. Will it be set against a wall, for example, and therefore only visible from the front and sides? Or is the intention for the display to be viewed all the way around? All of these elements influence the method you will use to contain your design. Several methods have been used in this book, each selected to work best for that particular arrangement. A step-by-step guide to each method follows. Read through and familiarize yourself with the process before starting your chosen design.

Free-Form Arrangement

The least complex technique is simply to arrange your stems freely in a vase to achieve a completely loose and natural display. This works well if you have large, heavy branches that will not fit through the holes in chicken wire or a pot-tape grid. Always start with the sturdier branches or stems, using them to form a grid-style frame within the vase. You can then place individual flowers within this grid-like structure and they will be held in place naturally by the interlocking stems. You can also follow these basic steps for hand-held bouquets.

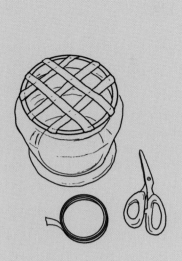

Pot-Tape Grid

Creating a grid of florist's pot tape across the top of a vessel, in a noughts and crosses style, can provide a great structure for an arrangement in a glass vase. This method avoids the need for a chicken-wire base, which would be unsightly through the transparent glass.

Materials

Clear vessel
Florist's pot tape
Strong scissors

Method

1. Make sure the vessel is completely clean and dry before you start, otherwise the tape may slip off the surface.
2. Cut several strands of tape long enough to span the opening of the vessel and place them at even intervals across the top. Work vertically and then horizontally to create a criss-cross grid pattern. Each square of the grid should be approximately 2 cm (1 in) square.
3. Use a small watering can or jug to pour the water through one of the holes to fill the vase until three-quarters full.
4. Now you can start designing. Simply place stems through the holes of the grid, using the tape to hold them in position.

Container with a Chicken-Wire Base

Most of the projects in this book rely on this method – it is by far my favourite. It is incredibly versatile and brings success no matter what shape, style or size a vessel is. The chicken wire acts as a mesh inside the container, into which the flower stems can be inserted. The resulting arrangement will always hold its shape.

Materials

Vessel of your choice
Chicken wire
Wire cutters
Gardening gloves
Florist's pot tape

Method

1. Once you have chosen your vessel, you can work out what size to cut your chicken wire. The best guide for this is to use a piece that is roughly four times the circumference of the vessel.
2. Scrunch the wire into a loose ball or brick, depending on the shape of your container, and place it inside the vessel. Wear gardening gloves to do this, as the wire may have sharp edges. Make sure the wire protrudes out of the vase a little.
3. Secure the wire in place with a few strips of florist's pot tape. Stretch them across the top of the vessel in a criss-cross pattern (see page 183).
4. Fill the vessel up to around three-quarters full with water using a jug or watering can. You are now ready to start your arrangement.

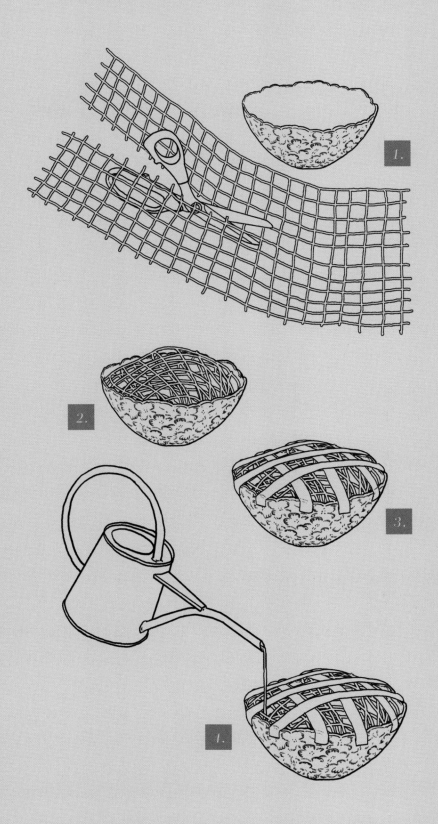

Chicken-Wire Structure for a Free-Standing Installation

This method uses chicken wire to create a structural support for very tall floral arrangements, such as Smoke & Grey on pages 66–71.

Materials

Vessel
Chicken wire
Wire cutters
Gardening gloves
Bamboo canes
Florist's pot tape

Method

1. Start by identifying where your structure will be placed in a room and decide on the height of the arrangement you are making.
2. Using wire cutters, cut a length of chicken wire that runs roughly from the top of your vase to the desired height of the finished design. Match the width of the chicken wire to that of the circumference of your vessel opening.
3. Roll the chicken wire into a tube shape and insert one end into the neck of the vessel. Wear gardening gloves to avoid catching your skin on any sharp ends of the cut wire.
4. You can insert a bamboo cane through the centre of the wire roll for extra stability. Secure this, and the chicken wire, in place using a few strips of florist's pot tape to make a criss-cross grid across the top of the vessel.
5. Once you have your structure secured, you can start to place the flowers. Create a guideline shape using the longest and bushiest branches, inserting the stems into the wire firmly to create a sturdy framework for the remaining stems.

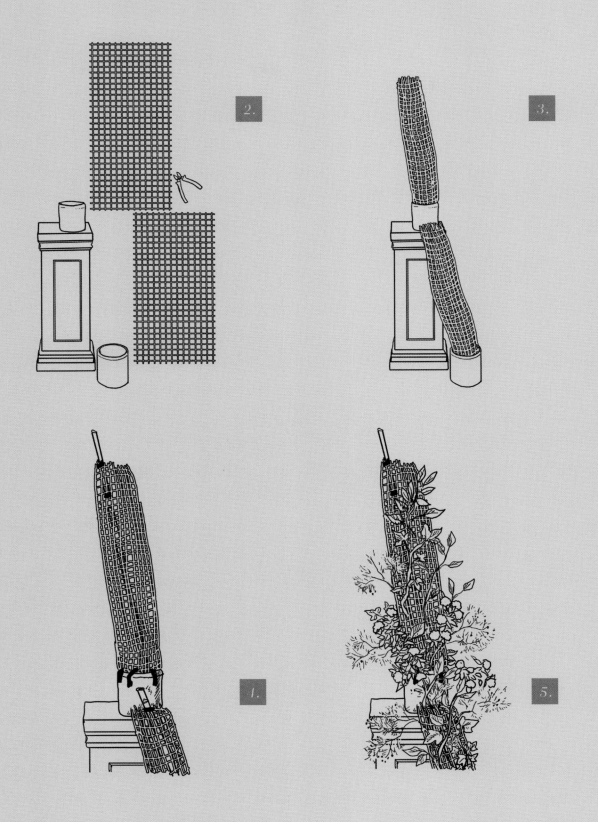

Chicken-Wire Structure for a Suspended Installation

This method uses chicken wire to create a structural shape for a hanging installation like the Moorland Cloud on pages 150–156. You will need a sturdy branch for the main support and suitable wall or ceiling fixtures from which to suspend the arrangement.

Materials

Sturdy branch
Wall or ceiling fixtures
Chicken wire
Wire cutters
Gardening gloves
Cable ties
Lightweight water
*   vessels (optional)*
Wire, rope or chain

Method

1. Choose a sturdy branch to which you can attach the chicken wire. If you are suspending it from existing wall or ceiling fittings, they need to be strong enough to take the weight of the entire arrangement.
2. Cut the desired length of chicken wire using wire cutters and then loosely scrunch and mould the chicken wire into a shape that is reflective of the finished piece. Wear gardening gloves to avoid catching your skin on any sharp ends of the cut wire.
3. Use cable ties to secure the wire to the branch, inserting the ties through the bunched-up wire and then passing them around the branch. Secure by pulling them as tight as possible. Repeat at regular intervals along the branch.
4. Hang the frame from your wall or ceiling fixtures using wire, rope or chain – whichever best suits the size, weight and style of the design.
5. With your structure suspended, you can begin to place the flowers and foliage. Start by creating a guideline shape using the longest and bushiest branches. Insert the stems into the wire firmly to create a framework for the remaining stems.
6. To cover larger areas, group bunches of stems together and tie them with string and cable-tie them to the chicken wire.

Stem Longevity

If using fresh flowers for a suspended arrangement, choose varieties that will last a whole day or more. A few lightweight vessels containing a little water can be placed upright within the chicken wire. Alternatively, stand individual flowers in test tubes of water taped in place. To avoid spillages, use a watering can or jug to fill containers with water once an arrangement is complete.

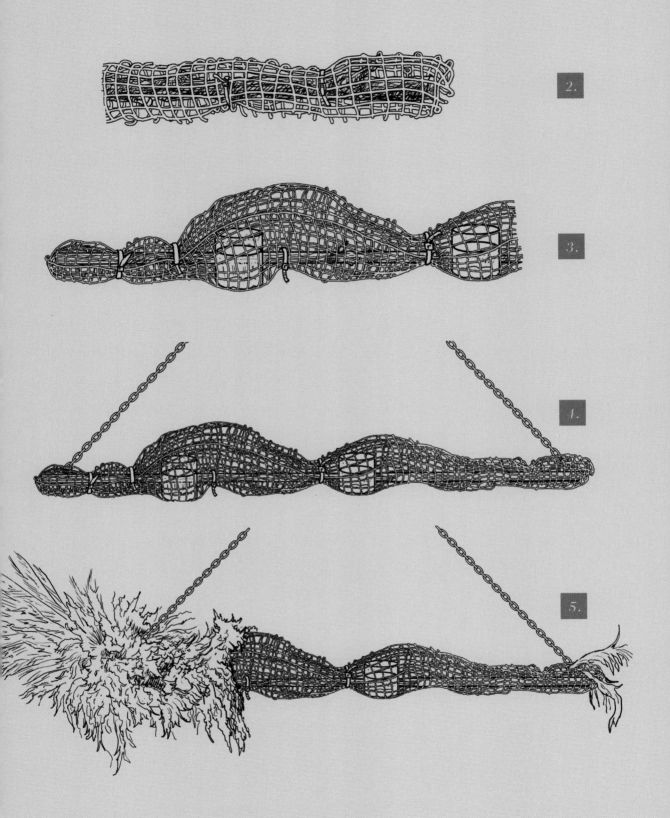

2.

3.

4.

5.

Making a Wreath

You can celebrate any season by adorning the walls and/or doors of your home with a wreath. You can give new life to a winter wreath by adding spring blooms and in autumn you can make the most of a wealth of evergreen foliage and berries. Experiment with a large-scale wreath like the one for All Hallows on pages 132–137.

Materials

Your choice of frame
Roll of wreath wire
Moss
Stems of choice
(flowers and
foliage), cut down
into smaller pieces
and florets
Wire cutters
Length of ribbon

Method

1. Start by tying the end of your roll of wire to the frame and securing with a knot. The wire will now stay attached for the entire wreath-making process.
2. If creating a moss base for an outdoor wreath, take a handful of moss and place it beside the spot at which the wire is attached. Hold on to the moss with one hand and use the other hand to wrap the wire around the moss and frame until it is secure. Repeat all the way around the frame until complete.
3. The following steps are identical for any type of wreath – indoor or outdoor. Work to create small bunches of your chosen stems, each the size of a hand span. Take three or four different types of stem for each bunch and place it flat onto the moss or straight onto the frame, starting at the point where you attached the wire in step 1.
4. Holding the bunch with one hand, use the other hand to wrap the wire around the wreath and the base of the stems until the bunch feels securely tied.
5. Continue to add bunches of stems in the same way, each time wrapping the wire just around the base of the stems. Layer all of the bunches in the same direction, gradually staggering them around the wreath. Aim to alternate one pointing slightly into the centre of the wreath and then one pointing slightly outwards.
6. As you work your way around the circle and get close to where you started, lift up your first bunch and tuck the last two beneath it, to give a seamless join.
7. Add a ribbon from which to hang your wreath, and any last decorative elements. Wrap a small wire around each item and poke it through the foliage and around the frame, turning the wire back on itself to secure.

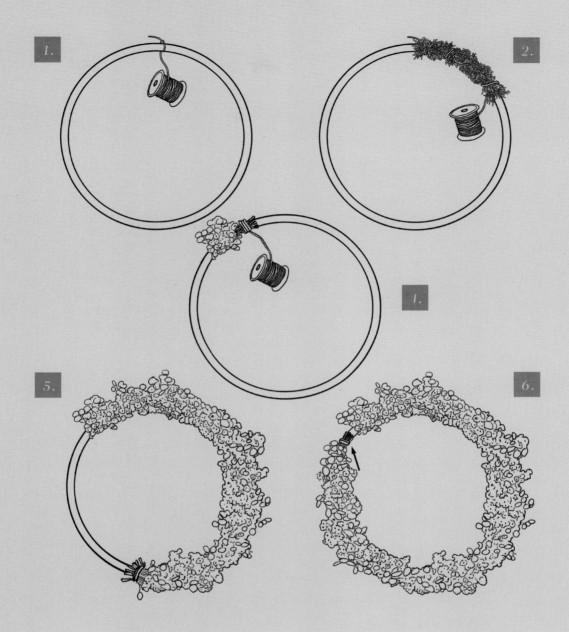

Choosing a Frame

A traditional moss-based frame is great for outdoors. Acting like a sponge, the moss soaks up moisture in the air, keeping the foliage and other natural ingredients fresher for longer. You can buy them in a local flower shop or craft store. For indoor wreaths, which inevitably dry out quicker, use either a wire frame (available from a florist's shop or wholesale) or a natural willow ring.

A BALANCED DESIGN

Flower arranging is an incredibly creative and expressive art. With flowers and foliage available in a huge variety of sizes, shapes and colours, there are literally no bounds. Your designs can be entirely of your own making. There are, however, a number of basic guidelines that will guarantee success every time.

The simplest rule is that an arrangement should be approximately two-thirds taller or wider (or a mix of both) than the vessel containing it. For this reason, you should choose a vessel carefully. It is easy to fall into the trap of creating something too tall in a shallow vessel, or selecting a large vase only to find you do not have adequate height in your chosen stems or enough bulk to fill it out. As a general rule, tall, narrow vessels will hold just a few tall stems or branches; medium-height vases with wide openings are great for bushier blooms and sheer volume; and small, low bottles and vases suit short or delicate single stems and flower heads.

Variety within an arrangement is also key. Aim to include several large-headed flowers to serve as focal points in the display. These can then be countered by a good number of medium- and smaller-headed flowers. Then you can consider extra height and texture, perhaps including foliage and/or seedheads.

Your Vessel Collection

A vessel is surprisingly significant in determining the overall effect of a finished design. Not only should you consider size, colour and shape, but also the material from which a vessel is made, its texture and even the atmosphere it creates. From large, antique-looking urns to rustic terracotta pots and from coloured glass vases to crackle-glazed ceramic bowls, your choice is infinite.

Types of Arrangement

There are many different types of arrangement available to you and the one you opt for in any given situation will depend on the blooms you have and the type of vessel you are using. Below are just a few ideas to help get you started.

Even balance

The most straightforward arrangement will have perfect symmetry all round, with the shape of the arrangement mirroring that of the vessel.

Trough style

In a long, low arrangement, it can work well to have big blousy focal flowers low down, towards the front of the arrangement, and tall wispy elements towards the back.

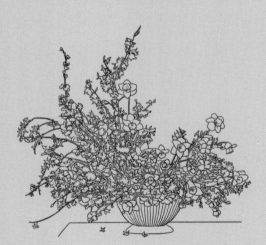

Asymmetry

You can create a more striking display by introducing a little asymmetry, with the highest and lowest point on opposite sides of the arrangement.

Statement display

Impressive, large-scale vessels can take extravagant displays that fulfil the two-thirds rule in both height and width and that feature a number of large focal blooms.

A FLOWER
THESAURUS

Depending on what you are creating and when, to select flowers for your own floral creations, or when swapping in different seasonal alternatives, it is useful to keep in mind the elements needed to create a well-balanced design. In most vase arrangements I work with the following categories:

- *Focal flower:* A large-headed bloom to take centre stage, such as a rose, ranunculus or peony.
- *Secondary flower:* Something to play alongside the leader, for example a smaller rose, tulip or echinacea.
- *Height and texture:* A few taller stems to achieve the highest points in the design. Forsythia, pussy willow, viburnum and smoke bush work well here. Texture could take the form of a whole world of seedheads, grasses and thistles.
- *Filler flower:* A smaller, more delicate or bushy flower to fill in spaces, that can be dotted around the arrangement, a little like seasoning. Anemones, zinnias and strawflowers are good examples.
- *Foliage:* Sometimes only very little foliage is necessary. I like to choose a selection of tonal varieties that are in keeping with the flower selection. Generally smaller, more delicate leaves work best, rather than anything too stiff and solid.

On the following pages, you'll find a selection of blooms that I find endlessly versatile. This is an unorthodox flower index, if you like, of favourite and too-often-forgotten flowers, ideas for pairings, benefits to the senses and mood, meanings.

Seasonal availability
Foliage year-round; berries and mauve/purple leaves November–February

Vase life
2 weeks

Uses
The bark of this plant yields a yellow dye, while the berries produce green and black colorants. Occasionally, the tender branches of common privet are employed to make baskets.

Privet
Ligustrum

Combine with
Hellebores and anemones for a winter vase arrangement

Seasonal availability
February–April

Vase life
1 week in bloom

Daffodil
Narcissus

Meaning
Rebirth and renewal. One of the first blooms of the year, the daffodil is celebrated for signs of new life.

Combine with
Most commonly enjoyed on their own en mass

Great Masterwort
Astrantia major

Meaning
The name *Astrantia* is derived from *aster*, which means 'star' in Latin. The name refers to the shape of the flower. In old folk tales the flowers are referred to as 'stars that have fallen to Earth'.

Seasonal availability
May–September

Vase life
2 weeks

Combine with
Ranunculus, garden rose and ammi for a summer garden arrangement

Fruiting Trees
Prunus

Seasonal availability
Blossom from March–May; Fruits from June–October, depending on variety

Vase life
1–4 weeks (depending on what stage blossom is at when cut)

Combine with
Tulips, Fritillaria and ranunculus for a spring celebration

Meaning
Cherry blossom is a particularly symbolic flower for spring, a time of renewal and new life. Its life is very short – around 2 weeks after peaking. It symbolizes the fleeting beauty of nature and transience of life.

ROSACEAE.

e abruptly, with the ends of the bony cells
Name from the Greek *mespilè*, a m r.)
18. CRATÆGUS (Hawthorn).—*Calyx* 5-cleft visions
acute ; *petals* 5 ; *styles* 1—5 ; *fruit* oval, or und, con-
cealing the ends of the bony cells. (Name om the
Greek *cratos*, strength, in allusion to the dness of
the wood.)

PRUNUS SPINOSA (Sloe, or Blackthorn)

1. PRUNUS (Plum and Cherry).

* *Fruit* covered with bloom; *young leaf* with
rolled together.

1. *P. communis* (Sloe, or Blackthorn ; Bullace and
Plum).—*Flowers* solitary or in pairs.—Under this name

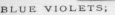

Combine with
Small delicate stems so they keep their value: muscari, blossom, iris, anemone

Violets & Primroses
Viola cornuta 'Tiger Eye Red' and Primula 'Blue Zebra'

BLUE VIOLETS;

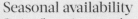

PRIMROSE
The Wild Poppy, or Corn Rose, is good to prevent falling sickness. The Syrup made with the leaves and flo is effectual in pleurisy, and St. Anthony's fire, or Erysip The dried leaves decocted have the same effect.

PRIMROSES.

Seasonal availability
Spring flowering – can be as early as February – and flower until summer

Vase life
3–4 days in tiny bud vases and glasses

Meaning
*With a name that derives from the Latin word **primus**, meaning 'first', primroses signify the first flower in spring. They are a symbol of renewal and new life. Trusty violets are a symbol of faithfulness, truth and loyalty.*

The dried fruit of the ... us Domestica, of the natural order ... much mucilaginous and saccharine matter ... and gently open the bowels, which they ... ating the passages and softening the excrement ... of great service in costiveness, accompanied with heat and irritation, which the more active cathartics would tend to aggravate. Where prunes are not

Seasonal availability
Fruits July–September; dark leaves from November–March

Vase life
2 weeks

Flower Stories
for

Little Gatherers

Meaning/uses
Folk names include bumble-kite, bounty thorn, skaldberry, blackbutter, blackbide, gatterberry, prickle thorn and dris-muine. Blackberries are a rich source of vitamin C, A, omega-3, potassium and calcium.

LONDON
JOHN F. SHAW AND CO.
.8 PATERNOSTER ROW

Bramble or Blackberry
Rubus fruticosus

Combine with
Anemones, hellebores, eucalyptus and privet for a wintery hedgerow look; remove thorns using scissors so they do not rip the more delicate petals in arrangements

Flowering Currant
Ribes sanguineum

Seasonal availability
Spring, March–May

Vase life
2 weeks

Use
A shrub usually found in parks and gardens, but often self-seeds in hedgerows and on waste ground. The flowers have a delicious floral flavour and can be added to salads or desserts.

Combine with
Tulips, ranunculus and peonies for a late spring/early summer arrangement

Mugwort
Artemisia vulgaris

Use
Mugwort holds many medicinal properties. The parts of the plant that grow above the ground are used to make essential oil. Compounds in the oil (including camphor, pinene and cineole) are said to have potent antioxidant, antibacterial and antifungal effects.

Seasonal availability
Flowers July–October

Vase life
Early in the season its flowers can easily wilt but in late summer/autumn, flowers can last for weeks and can be dried

Combine with
Grasses, seedheads and Japanese anemones for a late summer meadowscape

WILD FLOWERS
MONTH BY MONTH

Seasonal availability
May–September

Vase life
1–2 weeks fresh; can be dried as
an everlasting flower

Use
*In traditional Chinese medicine
bupleurum roots are a component
of the formula Free and Easy
Wanderer, which refers to the
Taoist concept of being able to go
with the flow of life.*

UMBELLIFEROUS TRIBE.   267

..., flat umbels of white flowers.—Fl. July,
... Perennial.
...*angustifolium* (Narrow-leaved Water Parsnep).—
...nnate; *leaflets* unequally cut, egg-shaped, the
...es narrower; *umbels* opposite the leaves,
...—Watery places; not unfrequent. Smaller than
...and resembling *Helosciadium nodiflorum*, from
...may be distinguished by its stalked *umbels*, and
...ving general and partial *bracts*, which are
...and often cut.

Combine with
Summer garden flowers

Thorow–Wax
Bupleurum rotundifolium

Meaning
*The name **Tanacetum** is derived from the Greek
word **athanasia**, which translates as 'immortal'.
The name probably refers to the plant's long
flowering period or its medical use*

Feverfew
Tanacetum

Combine with
*Herbs and wildflowers for
a summer meadow look*

Fever Few

Knapweed

Frogbit   Fluellin

Purging

Yellow Flag

Hogs Fennel   Flea Bane   Camomile

Seasonal availability
*Summer flowering,
May–September*

Vase life
2 weeks

Meaning
Every colour of rose holds a different meaning and numbers of stem can alter those meanings too. My favourite variety is the slightly dog-eared garden rose complete with dewdrops and a tiny snail.

Combine with
Bupleurum, ammi, astrantia and smoke bush

Rose
Rosa

ROSE TRIBE. 201

ROSA CANINA (Dog Rose)

R. arvensis (Trailing Dog Rose)... shoots feeble ; *leaves* smo... , not remaining attached to... ; *stigmas* forming a round head.—Woods an... ; common in the south of Engla... Distin... d from all the other British species of Rose by... der, trailing stems. The *flowers* are white and ... ess, and there are fewer prickles • than in most ... other species.—Fl. June—August. Shrub.

seed section
FIG. 44.—HIPS.

Seasonal availability
May–October

Vase life
1–2 weeks depending on variety

Meaning
Once considered a plant that would bring bad luck upon any house that takes the blossoms through its doors, this shrub is now considered more of a culinary and horticultural delight. Its bad reputation originates from its long, wickedly sharp thorns.

IDE AN... OOD... ND BLOSSOMS

SLOE BUS...
ground, are lon...
The stalks are...
leaves. The fi...
are small and ...
The seeds are s...
MEDICINAL...It is good for b...
in diarrhœa, ...
plied with grea...
into a poultice,...
ply it before the... it comes on...
Erysipelas. An ointment may be made of it for wounds.

SLOE BUSH.
Prunus Sylvestris. — It requires no description.
MEDICINAL VIRTUES.—All the parts of Sloe are astringent, and effectual to stay bleeding at the nose and mouth ; or bloody flux, profl... bowels, p... fruit to b... pose. T... and bowe... wash the ... kernels ... the head... water of ...

DESCR...
about dit...
Leaves n...
round, st...
the root, ...
in little ...
of a yello...

Blackthorn or Sloe
Prunus spinosa

Combine with
On their own in a tall vase

Seasonal availability
Blossoms early spring, February–April; fruits are best picked after a few frosts when they are ripe and soft

Vase life
1–2 weeks in bud to flowering

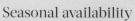

Hellebore

*Helleborus; Christmas
rose, Lenten rose*

Seasonal availability
*Winter flowering;
December–April*

Vase life
*If picked after the flower has
gone to seed, hellebores can
last 2–3 weeks in a vase.*

Combine with
*Narcissus, spirea, blossom and
other early spring flowers*

FIG. 81.—THE BEE.

Meaning
*In the Victorian language of flowers, hellebore refers
to a scandal, which fits well with the plant's links
to both witchcraft and insanity. But hellebore can
represent hope as well. It blooms in dark winter
days and reminds us that spring is on its way.*

HELLEBORUS VIRIDIS (Green Hellebore).

Combine with
*Mint, salvia, bupleurum and
chamomile for a scented summer
garden posy*

Self Heal

Seasonal availability
June–August; dried, year-round

Vase life
1 week as a fresh-cut flower

Lavender

Lavandula

Lovage   Lavender   Groundsell

Use
*Known for its properties for easing restlessness
and insomnia, lavender is widely used in
herbalism.*

Combine with
Perfect for wreaths and winter arrangements with seedheads, hellebores and twigs

Winter Evergreens
Cedrus, Juniperus, Pinus and Picea; *cedar, juniper, pine and spruce*

Meaning
Evergreens often symbolize immortality and eternal life because they retain their leaves/needles throughout the winter

Seasonal availability
All year

Vase life
3–4 weeks

Bracken
Pteridium

Seasonal availability
October–December; best once copper/rust-coloured

Vase life
Flatten under cardboard for 2 weeks after cutting to preserve its beautiful shape; it can then last months

Combine with
Big shaggy chrysanthemums and dahlias or in wreaths and winter arrangements

History
Fossil records indicate that bracken is a very ancient plant dating back 55 million years. Thought to be the most common plant in the world, it is found on all continents except Antarctica.

Ragwort & Sunshine

Senecio jacobaea and
Brachyglottis Sunshine

Meaning

Senecio means 'old man' in
Latin. This might refer to the
fact that *Senecio* often comes
in different shades of grey.

Seasonal availability

All year

Vase life

2–3 weeks

Combine with

A great staple foliage with a
sage-green to grey hue, this is great
as a soft-toned base for any
seasonal flower arrangement

Combine with

*Use on its own for a striking,
minimal, early spring arrangement.
Can be incredibly thorny, so is best
avoided with more delicate blooms.*

Seasonal availability

February–May

Vase life

2–3 weeks

Flowering quince

Chaenomeles

Meaning

*The name **Chaenomeles** comes from the Greek
words **chaino**, which means 'to divide', and
meles, which means 'apple', referring to the
fruit's form. The scientific name for this species is
speciosa, which means 'showy'.*

INDEX

About the Author & the Photographer

ANNA POTTER is an author and cofounder of Swallows & Damsons, a UK-based flower shop. Swallows & Damsons opened its doors in 2008 and has remained a little flower shop in the heart of the community, while contributing to international blogs and publications such as Design Sponge, Food 52, and Domino magazine. They have also designed for clients including Gucci, *Architectural Digest*, *Harper's Bazaar*, *The Telegraph*, and *Town & Country* magazine.

Known for bringing an unexpected and uniquely wild feel to floristry, Anna moves beyond the confines of blooms in floral decoration, incorporating a wealth of natural products and curiosities. Celebrating imperfections, subtlety in color and form in her designs, with inspiration from the rich darkness of Dutch still-life paintings, Swallows & Damsons is a modern-day influencer in a new wave of floral art and design.

INDIA HOBSON is a photographer who looks for the quieter moments in life, the beauty in the everyday and who celebrates conventionally overlooked corners. Ever drawn to the mystery of light and shadow and fascinated with exploring subtleties of colour, India has developed a distinctive style in her work, be it a portrait or still-life composition.

Clients include Burberry, Niwaki, Toast, *Kinfolk*, *HTSI*, *Architectural Digest*, *Condé Nast Traveller* as well as independent brands and individuals such as Pottery West, Campbell Cole, A Woven Plane and Pippins Denim.

India lives in Sheffield, UK.

Acknowledgements

So much gratitude to all the beautiful humans who made this book come to life.

Dan, thank you for providing the space just to be, and for offering limitless possibilities when I say there's only one way; for your ideas, love of nature, belief in the creative, and stillness; for seeing the difference between beauty and shiny bullshit and ruthlessly calling it; and for accepting both the light and the darkness and loving it all complete.

George, thank you for never pretending something is good when it's not; for your encouragement; and for doing the best impressions of me being a knobhead.

Albert, thank you for always bringing a spark and bright ideas, and for your boundless enthusiasm and wonder at small things. I love you all dearly.

India, thank you for working within the lines of a beautiful conversation so it never feels like work; for your raw feeling, seeing and being. I love spending time with you, the mind-blowing photos are always just a bonus.

Friends, family, thank you for letting me vent; for getting into the cold water with me; for bouncing ideas around and your eternal support.

To the best staff team: Alys, Louise, Jess, Kerrie, Erin, Vicky, Emma, Forest and Hannah. Thank you for never making me feel like any concept is unachievable and providing practical and logistical answers to problems. And thank you for being just really damn funny and wonderful to be around.

To all involved in the shoots and more . . . thank you!

Zara, Nikki Lee, Becky, Beth, Kirstin & Nick, Sam Binstead, Barra organics, Swim friends (Owen, Mick, Simeon, Adriano, Sian, Marnie, Bea, Gina, Roanna, Amy, Kate, Emma, Charlotte, Amie, Hannah, Frida, Lauren), Amy & Neil, Kat, Marigold and Larry, Magnus, Jan (field and bloom), Alfie (over the yardarm).

And, finally, thanks to Quarto for understanding the vision and for the opportunity to create this second book. Without your commitment, patience, hard work, and expertise it would not have been possible.

Brimming with creative inspiration, how-to projects, and useful information to enrich your everyday life, quarto.com is a favourite destination for those pursuing their interests and passions.

First published in 2023 by White Lion Publishing an imprint of The Quarto Group.
One Triptych Place, London, SE1 9SH,
United Kingdom
T (0)20 7700 6700
www.QuartoKnows.com

A catalogue record for this book is available from the British Library.

ISBN 978-0-7112-6857-9
EBOOK ISBN 978-0-7112-6859-3

10 9 8 7 6 5 4 3 2 1

Commissioning Editor *Zara Anvari*
Designer *Georgie Hewitt*
Editor *Anna Southgate*
Illustrator *Andrew Pinder*
Photographer *India Hobson*
Project Editor *Charlotte Frost*
Publisher *Jessica Axe*

Printed in China

Credits